About Michael Furtman

Michael Furtman has been a full time, freelance writer and photographer since 1982. He is the author of over twenty books, including Canoe Country Camping – Wilderness Skills for the Boundary Waters and Quetico.

His photographic work has graced many magazine interiors and covers.

You may view his books and photographs at www.michaelfurtman.com.

The New
BOUNDARY WATERS
AND QUETICO
FISHING GUIDE

MICHAEL FURTMAN

Birch Portage Press -- Duluth, MN

The New Boundary Waters and Quetico Fishing Guide
Michael Furtman

Birch Portage Press
Duluth, Minnesota

Front cover design and photos by Michael Furtman
Interior photos by Michael Furtman
Filleting diagrams by Allan Linne

Visit www.michaelfurtman.com

ISBN: 978-0-916691-05-9

0 9 8 7 6 5 4 3 2

Printed and bound in the United States of America

Dedication

*In memory of my father, Ralph Furtman,
who introduced me to the wonders of
the Canoe Country.*

Table of Contents

INTRODUCTION

Welcome to *The New Boundary Waters And Quetico Fishing Guide*, the updated edition of my classic title, *A Boundary Waters Fishing Guide*!

In case you're an owner of an earlier edition, and wondering if this version is worth the purchase, let me tell you that there is much new material in this book – new information on routes, new information on equipment, new information on fishing techniques, and a much more accurate and complete lake index. Lake information for both the BWCAW and Quetico has seen many changes and additions.

Yes, you'll find some familiar passages in this edition – no sense messing with a good thing! However, the number of changes and updates were so significant, that it required that I actually issue this as a new book, rather than a "revised" edition. There are two chapters that never appeared in the earlier book, and changes to every other chapter, some quite significant.

I first wrote this book in 1984. In fact, it was the first book I ever wrote. Since that time I've written over twenty books under my own name or ghost written, and I have to tell you that of them all, this little fishing guide has been my most consistent seller, and has remained in print the longest of any title. To say that I made a good choice in first writing this book is an understatement! I also quite enjoyed revisiting the old text, seeing what worked and what didn't, adding new advice, and updating the lake information. It caused me to recall quite vividly why I fell in love with the Canoe Country in the first place, and why it continues to draw me back each year. Today I find the portages a bit steeper and the packs a bit heavier than I did a few decades ago, but despite the increased aches and pains, there has never been a canoe trip I've regretted taking, nor has my passion to visit new lakes diminished. The Canoe Country is an enchanting mistress!

The longevity of this book probably shouldn't come as a surprise. The Canoe Country is a popular destination, and the U.S. side -- the Boundary Waters Canoe Area Wilderness -- is the most visited wilderness in the federal system. It has long stirred the imagination of anglers and canoeists, and will do so for years to come. Every year, new visitors plan their first trip, and in doing so, wonder how to fish the wilderness. Even experienced anglers find that fishing by canoe, in a remote area, presents challenges with which they are unfamiliar, or want to know what is in a particular lake, and so find this book of great use. For all those reasons, this little book has stayed in print for a nearly a quarter of a century! Amazing.

If you are purchasing this book, thank you. I hope you find it useful, informative, and well written. I also hope that you have a wonderful canoe trip.

Just a reminder – the wilderness is fragile. Please respect it, its fish and wildlife, and the other visitors you encounter. Given just a little care, we can preserve the wilderness, and the wilderness experience, for generations to come.

Michael Furtman
February 2008

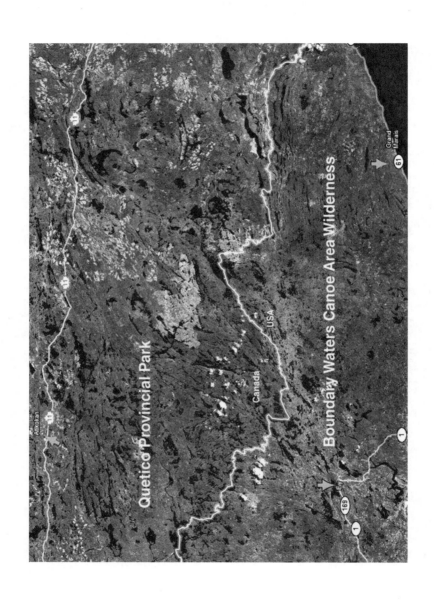

Goin' Up North

Large enough to feed one's imagination, the Boundary Waters Canoe Area Wilderness (BWCAW) and Quetico Provincial Park region is a haven for thousands of canoeists. They are also a haven for lots of fish. With over two million acres of woods and water and a border that extends for almost one hundred and fifty miles, the Quetico and Boundary Waters provide nearly unbounded opportunities for personal exploration. If one of your passions is fishing, the area is doubly blessed. Festooned with garlands of sparkling lakes, nearly each and every one containing fish, the Canoe Country can conjure up daydreams of large fish amongst even the least imaginative.

The first time I put foot and paddle into the Boundary Waters it was not known as such. At the time the American side's official moniker was the Superior Roadless Area, just a backwoods parcel of the Superior National Forest. We simply called it "goin' up north." Or, if in the mood to be a little more specific, we said we were going "close by Ely" or "up the Gunflint Trail." These references certainly date me. It's just that my family frequented the area often and my father, not one to let a bunch of kids interfere too much on his fishing, brought us along to feed the bugs. I was around five years old on the first trip that I can remember.

Our purpose in going "up north" was not just to canoe and camp. These were means to an end. The real reason we went there was to fish.

It was a long standing family tradition, dating back to the late 1940s, to make an early season lake trout trip. In those days the Minnesota lake trout season opened a bit earlier than it does now in order to take better advantage of the superb lake trout fishing to be had after the ice-out. At times we fished areas of a lake that had lost their ice only a matter of hours or days before our arrival, the rest of the lake sometimes still covered with the blue-black of rotting ice. Snow at night was not unusual and it was a fairly simple matter to find snow hidden in the shadows.

During those years, before the Boundary Waters was declared a wilderness area by law and motors were still being used throughout its length and breadth, fishermen were an extremely common group of visitors. While I suspect they enjoyed the scenery and pleasures of camping in this beautiful and rugged country no less than today's canoeing public, the main purpose of their trip was to fish. They came from all parts of this country to sample what truly was, and still is, some of the finest fishing anywhere.

Most of these people were experienced fishermen and those that were not hired one of the many fishing guides that made their livelihood in this land of woods and water. Because they were coming to fish first and camp second, they were well prepared with the tackle and knowledge needed to take their catch. And because they had motors to do the work, they could lug along a few extra pounds of fishing gear, not to mention the extra ease of fishing from a motor powered canoe. Little time was wasted on waters they knew nothing about.

Today, things are different. With the declaration of a wilderness status for the Boundary Waters in 1978, and the near elimination of the use of outboard motors in the BWCAW and Quetico, more and more of the area's visitors are there to enjoy the special solitude and remoteness. You could watch the change in the user groups as each phase of the restrictions on motor routes was implemented. Gradually, visitors came to canoe and camp first, and fishing became a secondary concern.

This is as it should be. While the Canoe Country's fishing is undeniably a big attraction, it is the magic of wilderness that embodies the region's true value. One may find fishing in many places; the tonic of expansive solitude is a much rarer commodity.

Still, to someone who had fished this area for years it came as quite a shock to find people up there who couldn't give a hoot about fishing. Equally as confusing was seeing folks who had fishing equipment with them but had assembled such a poor array as to be virtually worthless.

Once, after completing the portage into a favorite lake trout lake, Mary Jo and I strung up our rods and decided to do a little trolling on our way

to select a campsite. We were lucky enough to pick up a half dozen lakers as we paddled along but, when we rounded the bend near the campsite of our choice, we found it occupied.

Disheartened, we turned the canoe down the lake. As we began to get turned around, we latched on to a dandy lake trout. All activity ceased except for the fight and there was more than usual interest by the group watching us from the campsite we had hoped to use. When the fish began to tire, and we eased it up to the canoe, one of the camp's occupants apparently could stand it no longer. He slid his canoe into the lake and paddled furiously out to us. As he neared, he called out, "What didja catch?"

"A nice laker," I replied, "it's the seventh one today."

"Geez," he returned chagrinned, "we've been fishin' this lake for six days for walleyes and haven't caught a one, let alone a lake trout."

Now I don't like to play one-upmanship, but I thought maybe he would like to know. "It doesn't surprise me that you haven't caught any walleyes, there aren't any in this lake, nor within four portages. It is a good lake trout lake though."

He never said a word. Turning his canoe around he paddled back to his camp shaking his head. I don't know if he caught any lakers after that. I hope he did.

You don't have to be that confused to not catch fish. Many of the individuals that canoe this area hope to catch a few fish along the way and may have a fair idea of what kind of fish to expect on their route. But fishing in Lake Minnesewer back home is often much different than fishing up north. Sitting at home and planning a trip to this area can conjure up dreams of big fish and fresh filleted shore lunches. Knowing what to do and what to use once you get there, well, that can be quite different than what you had foreseen.

On a trip long ago, one that I thought I had carefully researched, we were nearly flummoxed. Mary Jo, my brother Greg, and friend Bill Rudie were to be out for six days, alternately camping then moving on each day. I knew that we wanted to camp on lakes X, Y and Z so I dutifully found out as much as I could about the fishing in each of those lakes. I was not too concerned about the lakes we planned merely to cross. You know what they say about the best laid plans of mice and men.

Nearing the end of the trip we were caught in a terrible thunder and lightning storm. We quickly made for shore, and as the storm seemed to be a large one with no end in sight, we madly set up camp. It blew and rained the rest of the day with the miserable precipitation finally letting up about supper time. Grateful for the chance to make a quick dinner, we piled out of the tents and grabbed the food bag. Somehow, in the confusion of the cloudburst, the stuff sack containing the food had not been put under shelter. The only things salvageable were some spaghetti noodles and the peanut butter. My wife threatened to make a peanut butter sauce to go with the spaghetti. I decided to go fishing.

The wind was still whistling fiercely down the length of the lake, whitecaps building to near three feet as they approached our campsite on the point. Desperate for an edible dinner, I tried fishing from shore. Three things quickly became evident. The wind was too strong to cast into on the windward side of the point and the water too shallow on the lee side. The third thing was that, since we had not planned on fishing this lake, let alone camp on it, I did not bother to find out what was in it. Dejectedly, I walked back to camp. My wife was beginning to make the peanut butter sauce for the noodles.

To make a long story short, if that is still possible, I decided it was calm enough on the lee side of the point to slide the canoe out into a little deeper water. With one man handling the canoe while the other fished, it was barely possible to keep from capsizing. Now all I had to do was figure out how to catch whatever might be in this lake.

The lakes surrounding this one had either lake trout or smallmouth bass in them. A few had both. I decided it looked more like a smallmouth lake than a trout lake and made my tackle selection. I tied a top water plug. Nothing. I put on a shallow running plug. Zilch. I tried on a jig. Zero. Spoons and spinners produced the same results. I went to live bait and tried a leech and floating jig combination. No strikes. Finally I put on a small bait hook and a plain leech.

The area we could fish, because of the strong wind, was small. It looked good, and because it was the only spot we could fish and I wasn't optimistic about the palatability of the concoction simmering in camp, I fished it thoroughly with each new selection from the tackle box.

On the very next cast I felt a tremendous strike. Perhaps it was that I really didn't expect to catch anything at this point, but I missed on the set. Rebaiting the hook, I tossed it into the same spot, this time to hook the fish. When I set the hook, a green slab leapt skyward. A bass! So I was right, I thought, there are smallmouth in this lake. It wasn't until I boated the fish that I realized my mistake.

Friends, there is only one thing scarcer than a honest politician and that's a largemouth bass in the Boundary Waters. But that is what this fish was, and so was the next.

Though I was surprised by their presence, I was grateful for it. With a couple of three pound bass I had enough (barely) to feed the four of us and forego the peanut butter pasta. I then and there decided to learn more about what was in the lakes of the Boundary Waters, and that was the beginning of this book.

With all the lakes in this wonderful area, even if you have fished it for years, there is no way one could know them all. Nights spent pouring over maps only serve to set the fishing juices flowing. It is a marvelous thing to have a vivid imagination but does little to improve your fishing.

Because there are so many lakes in the Canoe Country and because much of the time we are only on a particular lake for a short time, many do not do the research necessary to find out just what is in the lake or what it is like.

Those of us who frequent the area probably have a favorite lake or two. Not because these lakes are exceptional fishing lakes. Many times it is just because we are familiar and comfortable with the lake. Our trips are valuable to us and we don't want to waste time in an area that may not be up to par. Finding out about other lakes is not always easy. Even the best of friends will lie straight faced when asked about a good lake. For those who do not live in the immediate area surrounding the Canoe Country, there are no friendly bait shops to give hints and the nearest

Fisheries Office of the Minnesota DNR or Ontario Ministry of Natural Resources may not be known to them.

These then are the reasons for this book. Too much of modern fishing literature is centered on high-tech fishing techniques. This guide will tell you the basics about both the lakes you will encounter and the habits of the fish. It hopes to inform the reader about the tackle requirements for the changing lakes and species you will fish for as you paddle through and how to put the kit together so that it is still portageable.

It won't make you a fishing expert. Nor do you need to be an expert to catch fish in the Canoe Country. You don't need a degree in limnology or have to own all the latest in electronic fishing paraphernalia to catch fish.

Knowing how to read a lake, where to look for fish, what their habits are and how to present the lure are far more important than all the edges modern equipment and do-dads may profess to give. Hopefully this guide book will verse you upon these basics, teach you a little something about the lakes and their fish.

When I first fished the Canoe Country with my father many years ago our success was sometimes fantastic. It still can be. It is one of the major reasons I return there as often as I do. The pristine lakes and bountiful fish are relatively unchanged and the country offers greater rewards than numbers of dead fish. Maybe, armed with the basic tackle and knowledge we need we can all take a fishing trip back into what still is the "good old days."

I hope you find this book a valuable aid in catching a fine mess of fish.

When And Where To Go

Timing Is Everything -- For Anglers

The canoe country of the Boundary Waters and Quetico offers some of the finest angling anywhere. One of the great benefits of this area's wilderness designation is that the lakes receive relatively low angling pressure, and few people pack fish out, preferring to keep just a few for meals while on their adventure.

Because of this, fish populations are healthy, but it doesn't mean that they exactly jump into your canoe or boat. Like angling anywhere, timing is everything, and to enjoy the best results, anglers should fish for the right species during the right month.

Ice-out in the Canoe Country is about the first week of May, at least in an average year, and Minnesota's fishing season opens shortly thereafter. If you're headed into the Quetico for early lake trout, you need not worry about when the season opens. While walleyes will still be off limits, lake trout can be legally taken in Ontario as soon as the ice is out.

Whether you're in the BWCAW or Quetico, once the walleye seasons are open, the majority of anglers will be chasing walleyes. But as far as I'm concerned, the best angling in the Canoe Country in May is for lake trout.

At no other time of the year will lakers be so easy to catch. Sensitive to both light and temperature, these fish dive toward the bottom as waters warm and days lengthen. But during May, and even into June during some cool years, anglers can expect to catch lakers in the shallows, from the surface to twenty feet deep. Contrast this to July and August, when the trout plunge to forty feet or more in depth.

On the heels of laker fishing comes the best time to pursue smallmouth. In the Canoe Country, smallies are on their spawning beds in early June, and remain shallow until about the Fourth of July to take advantage of mayfly hatches. The surface fishing can be spectacular, whether you use spinning gear and plugs like the Heddon Tiny Torpedo, or fly fish with bass bugs or big dry flies that imitate the monster Hexagenia mayfly. Concentrate your efforts near fallen trees that extend out over rocky rubble bottoms and hold on.

By July, the lake trout fishing really slows, and smallmouth begin to move deeper (though the smallies can still be readily taken on diving plugs or leeches fished on a walleye type rig). Most anglers prefer to fish for walleyes during the latter half of May and through June, but I generally ignore walleyes during this period in favor of lake trout or bass, since this is the period best for these two species. After all, walleye fishing in the Canoe Country holds up well all through the summer.

The reasons are simple. Because these lakes are pretty far north, many tend to avoid the "dog days" walleye fishing syndrome synonymous with warm weather. Since the lakes tend to stay cooler, even into late August, walleyes can be found in water less than fifteen feet deep.

This is especially true on the large lakes of the international border, or any of Quetico's lakes that form part of the Hunter's Island canoe route (i.e., Kawnipi, Sturgeon, etc.), because these lakes are essentially part of one large flowage. Strong currents move through narrows in these lakes, and this moving water is well oxygenated and carries foods. Even smaller lakes that are part of a river system hold up well. I've found while on several mid-August trips to just such lakes, walleyes were abundant and feeding heavily, taking jigs fished in water only ten feet deep. By concentrating your efforts on such flowages, you can avoid the "light-bite" syndrome so common with late summer walleyes.

If it sounds like I've ignored northern pike all summer, you're mistaken. Plenty are taken while fishing for these other species. But if you want to target BIG northerns, I'd recommend heading out in late August and into

September. Fall comes early to the canoe country, and the red splash of moose maples appears before August ends. As these lakes begin to cool, northerns return to the shallows to chase small baitfish like wolves rounding up prey. Large stick baits and big Mepps-type musky spinners, either cast or trolled, can provide awesome angling. The best areas I've found are where these horsetail reeds and other vegetation abuts rocky, windy points. The reeds provide pike a place to hide for their ambush attack style.

I suspect that, like me, your favorite fish is the one currently on the end of your line. But by targeting a particular species during a particular month, you can help make sure that your canoe trip combines great angling with a great wilderness experience.

Where to go is a different matter entirely. The end of this book contains an index to most of the lakes in the twin wilderness areas, so prior to your departure, you'll have a good idea of what is in the lakes you'll be visiting. But few canoe trips are designed solely around fishing. There may be many other factors involved.

Planning And Priorities -- Keys To A Great Canoe Trip

It's pretty hard to have a bad visit to the Canoe Country, but every year I hear stories of people who managed to do just that.

But what does it take to have a great canoe trip? Each year I get dozens of inquiries from readers of my books and articles asking me for advice on planning a trip, choosing a time of year, or selecting an entry point and route. What follows is the advice I give virtually everyone who writes.

Just what is it you want your canoe trip to deliver? Sounds simple, but it really isn't. Few routes can deliver on everything, so talk to your intended canoeing partners to see just what it is you want to experience. If most or all are avid anglers, a route that takes you to the better fishing lakes (not every lake provides good fishing) is in order. Not only that, but if they want to target a particular species, such as lake trout to the exclusion of other species, that desire will not only affect where you go, but when. For instance, the best lake trout fishing is in May, while the best smallmouth fishing is in June. The worst fishing for everything is in August. In other words, if angling is your interest, routes and timing need to be designed around that.

Or are you seeking the ultimate in solitude? Not every route offers the kind of peace and quiet you may seek. Some routes, especially during the peak visitation period of mid-July to mid-August will be positively busy (a relative term, I know) but offer more solitude at a different time of year.

You don't need the fanciest gear to go into the wilderness, but you do need good gear. If you've never done a wilderness canoe trip before, I strongly recommend you contact one of the outfitters that cater to Canoe Country visitors. Not only can they help you in getting permits and selecting routes, they all have quality tents, canoes, packs and other needed gear. It is my opinion that the outfitters in northern Minnesota are the best in the business.

Renting gear is a great way to see what works, and why, without having to make a purchase investment. For instance, you may have been eyeing that fancy backpack at a store, but by first renting you'll quickly learn just why the venerable old Duluth-style pack is superior for canoe travel.

If you want to outfit yourself, that's great. Just make sure you do a little research first. There are several good books available, such as my own *Canoe Country Camping* (University of MN Press), that explain what kind of gear works best. It's easy enough to buy something these days that will disappoint you on the trail. Spend some time reading up on it.

Finally, leave about half the stuff you'd like to take at home. Pare down your gear to the minimum needed. Nothing will ruin a canoe trip faster than laboring over portages all day because you've hauled too much stuff. You want to be fishing, reading a book, or watching the clouds drift by, not struggling like a Sherpa on Everest.

In a nutshell, the very best advice I can give is to PLAN. Plan carefully, talk to those who are more experienced than yourself, read some good books on the subject and use the services of an area outfitter when required.

Another consideration is whether to head into the Boundary Waters or the Quetico. It may be assumed by some that the fishing is better in the Quetico because getting there is more difficult, and the park only allows in about one-quarter the number of visitors than is allowed in the Boundary Waters.

I'll give you a tip. I think the two very best fishing lakes in the Canoe Country are Kawnipi and Crooked lakes. The first one is in the Quetico, the second, largely in the Boundary Waters (though on the international border). In other words, just being north or south of the imaginary line that is the international border doesn't automatically make a lake better or worse for fishing. A lake's characteristics are most important.

Fishing pressure in the Canoe Country is relative – yes, some lakes get hit a lot harder than others. But all of them get fished a lot less than lakes outside the wilderness boundaries. Few fish are kept within the wilderness, usually just enough for a meal.

So what does this all mean? Excellent fishing can be had on either side of the border. If someone put a gun to my head and made me choose one side or the other, I guess I'd have to pick the Quetico because, on the whole, there are more big lakes, and these big lakes are very fertile and productive fisheries. And solitude, something I cherish, is easier to find on the Canadian side. That said, there are many excellent places to fish in the Boundary Waters, and my quick fix lakes are all on the U.S. side.

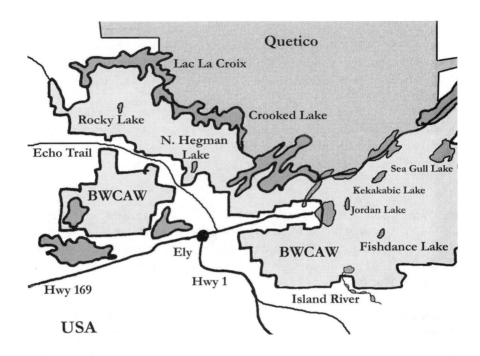

BWCAW VS. QUETICO

There is mystery surrounding the Quetico, that northern half of the beloved Canoe Country. To many it signifies an ideal, what they wish the Boundary Waters could be. For these people, the Quetico is a place of solitude, of exploration, of magic. Others are intimidated by the Quetico. They see it as possibly too remote, a place where they fear they will be tested beyond their abilities. They've heard stories of difficult routes or portages that are hard to find.

In reality, the Quetico is probably both. It does indeed offer more solitude than the Boundary Waters. There are more "off the beaten track" routes. And yes, sometimes on these routes, portages can be difficult to find and traverse. Invariably, every visitor to the canoe country will begin to compare the two wilderness areas. In many regards the two are very similar, but their differences are also quite real.

Both are the epitome of Canoe Country. By far, the majority of portages are short, and the routes seemingly endless. Both share the beauty of the Canadian Shield, the sweeping granite underpinnings of that part of the world. Though some of the flora in the south central part of the Boundary Waters is more deciduous, much of the habitat and topography of the Boundary Waters and Quetico is very similar. Aside from the Forest Service firegrates, most Boundary Waters campsites could be easily mistaken for a site in the Quetico.

Perhaps the biggest reason for differences between the two wilderness areas lies in political boundaries. Take a look at a map. The Boundary Waters is long (east to west) and narrow (north to south). Quetico Provincial Park, however, is about as wide as it is long. Though both contain nearly the same acreage, about one million acres apiece, how that acreage is shaped plays a considerable impact on its use. And use contributes mightily to how we perceive each.

While there are seldom used routes in the Boundary Waters, its narrowness allows most of the best of it to be easily penetrated in not much more than a day. In other words, should you enter from a point on the west, by the time you thought you should be getting away from folks, you probably will begin encountering other visitors that have entered from east of you. Most visitors to the Boundary Waters spend four days on their trip, and should they want to, there are very few areas they can't traverse in that period of time. If they do, it won't be without encountering parties coming the opposite direction from another entry point.

Even the international border route is fragmented, for along the eastern third, Magnetic, Gunflint and North Lakes lie outside the Boundary Waters, and the Canadian half of all lakes east of Saganaga are not in the Quetico, and therefore do not have wilderness protection. This results in the confusing situation where motors are allowed on one side of a lake (Canadian), and not on the U.S. side (those within the BWCAW), and on both sides of some.

Combine this with the fact that skilled paddlers, or those who use motor routes, can penetrate very far into the Boundary Waters on just a day trip, and the perception of heavy use is increased.

When my wife Mary Jo and I were stationed as volunteer Wilderness Rangers on Crooked Lake, we encountered a few folks who had come in that fairly substantial distance just for the day. On peripheral lakes day use can be heavy. This is not to say that such use is right or wrong, just that it does quantify one big difference between the two wilderness areas.

The Boundary Waters is not only surrounded by roads, it is also dissected by them, and these roads feed numerous access points. This plethora of entry points effectively eliminates the possibility of substantial portions being remote. The BWCAW is divided into three sections: that portion east of the Gunflint trail; that section west of it, stretching beyond Ely to Crane Lake; and that part south of the Echo Trail. While it is still possible to plan a canoe trip that takes you from one section to another, such routes require leaving the wilderness and crossing one or more roads, a factor that decreases the perception of remoteness, and also means running into more folks who are entering from access points serviced by those roads. Consequently, remoteness can be a hard to find commodity in the Boundary Waters. Exceptions would be lakes in the northern part of that thumb of land jutting into Lac La Croix, or that central part of the BWCAW north of Polly Lake and south of Knife. Most of the truly remote spots in the BWCAW are on dead end routes and on very small lakes.

Now take a look at the Quetico. It is buffered on the south by the Boundary Waters. There are no roads leading to either the west or east sides. While access is good from the north, most Canadians choose to recreate elsewhere (over 80% of Quetico visitors are Americans), and the human population to the north of Quetico is small. The drive time to these northern Quetico entry points easily adds another three hours (versus Ely, for instance), which makes them less attractive to many Americans, especially those pressed for time or already driving a long distance.

QUETICO OR BWCAW?

-- QUETICO OFFERS GREATER SOLITUDE.

-- BWCAW OFFERS EASIER ACCESS.

-- PERMITS ARE HARDER TO GET FOR QUETICO.

-- BWCAW IS BETTER FOR DAY TRIPS.

-- QUETICO IS MORE EXPENSIVE TO VISIT.

-- FISHING IS EQUALLY GOOD!

Quetico also offers many circle route opportunities that pass through seldom visited sections, and there are huge lakes and long rivers that are entirely within the park. Most of the large lakes in the Boundary Waters are shared with motors or fall on busy travel routes. Remote BWCAW routes are almost just side trips, taking at the most a day or two to traverse.

Finally, a Quetico visitor from outside Canada must first stop at a ranger station within the park to pick up their permit, as opposed to the Boundary Waters, where you pick up your permit at a Forest Service office or outfitter outside the park. Stopping at a Quetico ranger station is easily done at the Prairie Portage (south central Quetico/ BWCAW border). It is somewhat more difficult from the Saganaga Lake end. The situation to the far west is even more difficult as permits must be picked up at the Ranger station on Lac La Croix. This adds up to much, much lower day use, and a weeding out, of sorts, of many people who just don't want to invest the extra time or money in visiting the Quetico. In other words, just getting to the Quetico takes more time and effort, which tends to decrease the number of visitors and increase solitude. Finally, Quetico issues far fewer permits than does the Forest Service for the Boundary Waters. Even if access issues were identical, use of Quetico would, because of the availability of permits, always be lower.

In 1985, Mary Jo and I spent thirty days, from late July to late August, wandering the Canoe Country. We entered from Beaverhouse Lake on Quetico's northwest corner and exited at Ely. Despite the fact that this is the heaviest use period of the year, we experienced in the Quetico two five day segments where we never encountered another human. And

until we reached the Boundary Waters, even on those days when we saw other visitors, the numbers were low. On many nights we camped in sites that appeared to have been unused not only that year, but perhaps for a quite a few years. We were able to travel down routes where portages were not much more than game trails, where we felt as though we were the first to pass that way.

It really takes no more skill to visit the Quetico than it does the Boundary Waters. The routes, though more remote, can be easily traveled by even the least experienced. So whether you choose the Boundary Waters or Quetico, fear not that either is beyond your ability. Fishing can be excellent on both sides of the boundary. The difference is largely in the amount of other people you'll see. Expect to see folks on the U.S. side fairly frequently. Expect the opposite in most parts of the Quetico.

BWCAW Routes

If solitude is also an important part of your fishing trip, and yet you're not ready to visit the Quetico, there are areas in the Boundary Waters that offer it. Finding these places takes work and planning and requires travel through busier areas to get to and from them. But the rewards are there for those willing to make the effort.

In all my years of writing about and working in the BWCAW, one particular question from readers and visitors stands out: "Can you recommend a loop with short, easy portages, nice campsites, good fishing, and where we won't see many other people?" The question would be comical if it weren't so common. The answer, of course, is no. Which should give you some clues as to how to get away.

Routes to small lakes with little reputation, routes with frequent, and occasionally long, portages, and routes that dead end are the keys to finding solitude. You also need to be a bit smarter than the average tourist so that you can recognize these areas, as well as to minimize your gear and load so you can travel a bit faster and further.

The last point is very important. The average visitor spends four days in the BWCAW. Mostly, they go in as far as they can before exhaustion sets in from hauling enormous loads, set up camp, and stay there for the entire trip. Which means those of us willing to go a little further and faster, and willing to travel each day, can hit the more remote areas.

Remember, on all of the routes I'll recommend, you will encounter a fair number of people on at least your first and last days. Pay close attention to your maps to find campsites in back bays, on small lakes one portage off the main route, or beyond a particularly long portage. By doing so, and traveling midweek, you might just avoid crowds.

The Thumb of Lac La Croix Route

Protruding north into sprawling Lac La Croix on the far west of the BWCAW is a large peninsula of land. While La Croix is gorgeous, it is also well visited by paddlers (especially on the east end), and is motorized on the Canadian half. But the peninsula around which La Croix is wrapped offers beauty and serenity.

Visitors should acquire an entry permit for the Little Indian Sioux entry point on the Echo Trail. An easy day will take you down the river, which is full of wild rice and often visited by waterfowl and moose, through Upper and Lower Pauness lakes to the portage around the Devil's Cascade. You'll encounter four relatively short and easy portages before reaching this 160 rod (a rod is 16 1/2 feet) trail. At the end of this trail is Loon Lake. Though Loon is motorized, the traffic level is low. On this day you will likely see the most people of your trip.

From here you have some choices: spend the first night on Loon Lake or continue on over the Beatty Portage (a railroad track marine portage for hauling boats into La Croix) before stopping for the night. Your choice will depend on whether you will enter the thumb of La Croix via Loon Lake or from La Croix.

Either route will open up the interior. From Loon Lake, exit east out of East Loon Bay, to Little Loon and then Slim lakes. Though the maps don't show it, there is a little used portage between Slim and Fat lakes going east. You could also exit Slim via Section 3 pond, and cut east again at North Lake.

Or you could enter North Lake by continuing down La Croix to Snow Bay. This will give you a chance to experience this big, lovely lake, and see some pictographs on the east shore just beyond Beatty Portage, before hitting the hinterlands. By the end of day two, in either case, you should be well into the interior.

A look at the maps will show a bunch of lakes to explore as you wander east. They are all lovely and the choice is yours. The only other decision you'll need to make upon reaching Pocket Lake is whether to exit back onto La Croix on the east end, or veer south through Gebeonequet Lake. The latter will be more lonely.

Finally, no matter how you wind around, you'll need to head for Oyster Lake and begin working west through a chain of small lakes that, though somewhat more visited than those you've just passed through, are relatively lightly used. Once you reach Shell Lake and portage south out of it, you're back on the Pauness lakes and the river route back to your car.

At the least, four days should be planned for this trip. Five is more realistic. Although many of the small lakes on this route are incredibly scenic, I wouldn't recommend them for fishing destinations. However, some of the medium-sized lakes offer excellent walleye and bass fishing, and there's even a secret brook trout lake near this route.

Escape From Lake One

Lake One is a busy place. The lakes the follow it (Two, Three and Four) aren't a whole lot better. They all meet the requirements of the "common question", and use shows it.

But since those folks who adhere to the tenants of that question rarely venture far afield, there is hope. Surrounding these lovely but busy lakes are interesting side routes that can offer some serious solitude.

For instance, from the southeast corner of Lake Three you can portage to Horseshoe Lake and beyond to North and South Wilder. After a night there, you can exit north to Hudson Lake, crossing the busy route to Insula Lake, and continue north to Fire Lake, then west to Delta and

Rifle. Or once on Hudson Lake you could go with the flow east to Insula and then dive into the bush by heading south to Hope and South Hope lakes and eventually to very remote Maniwaki. This dead end path is seldom used.

Almost every lake in this part of the Boundary Waters provides good to excellent fishing, even the busy lakes One, Two and Three. There are a couple of seldom visited lakes in this part of the Boundary Waters where I've had not just good, but truly exceptional walleye angling.

Heart of the Boundary Waters Route

If there is a truly remote area in the BWCAW, it is in that part of the wilderness lying north of the Kawishiwi Lake entry point, and south of Kekekabic Lake. This area is the furthest possible distance from any entry point, and though not unused, is generally only visited by those with more than four days on their hands.

With a permit in hand for Kawishiwi Lake entry point (west of the Sawbill Trail), you head north through a chain of lakes (Kawishiwi, Square, Kawaschachong, etc.) and creeks along a well visited route. However, if you can reach Malberg Lake your first day, you'll leave a fair share of your company behind on overused Lake Polly.

Once on Malberg you can head northeast through an interesting route toward Little Saganaga Lake (a fairly popular spot), or you can exit Malberg to the west down the Kawishiwi River (which really is more of a long meandering lake). Lying north of the river, or west of the chain of lakes heading toward Little Sag are a bunch of small and medium sized lakes that receive only nominal visitation. You can make a nice loop by heading north toward Little Sag, steering west at Makwa Lake and then eventually heading south to Malberg via Boulder, Adams and Elbow lakes. There are also numerous dead end routes here that probably offer the best escape, since most folks don't like retracing their steps.

Besides being a somewhat remote route, this area provides some excellent fishing for walleye and northern pike. I've even found a few lakes with some jumbo bluegills in this region, and a few that can supply a largemouth bass or two. Only recently have smallmouth bass begun to pioneer some of the lakes along this route, and time will tell if they become good smallmouth fisheries.

I won't tell you too much more for fear of meeting all of you on a favorite lake. Besides, exploration is half the fun.

West From Burntside Lake

Majestic Burntside Lake, on the edge of Ely and outside of the BWCAW, is your path to the Crab Lake entry point along Burntside's west shore. Though Crab Lake itself receives a fair amount of use, as does larger Cummings Lake beyond it, this area provides a good chance to get away for two reasons: long portages and many small lakes with single campsites.

Long portages scare people, even though the ones in this area are flat and easy. Because the portages are feared, you'll find most visitors camped on Cummings and Crab lakes. Couple that with the fact that many of the small lakes beyond those portages have only a single campsite and you'll start to feel like you're really alone. There are a few small lakes north of Cummings that are so rarely visited that you'll have a hard time finding the portages. Have fun exploring!

This region also provides some good fishing opportunities, especially for smallmouth bass. I'm not going to give away any secrets here, but I will tell you that as a fishing destination, several lakes in this part of the Boundary Waters are top notch!

The true beauty of the Canoe Country is that there are so doggone many choices. I've paddled and portaged the region now for nearly half a century, and still there remains lakes I've not visited, routes I've not traveled and fish I've not caught! How very wonderful that is for all of us.

Thank goodness wise men and women had the foresight to set these two special wilderness areas aside for all of us to enjoy. You may enter the wilderness intent on finding great fishing, but no matter if the fish bite or not, I can guarantee that you will arrive back home a changed person. The magic of the Canoe Country is that strong.

So go ahead. Pick an entry point. Research the fish in the lakes beyond that entry point with this book. Stock up on the tackle recommended, and venture forth.

You may or may not find the fish you desire, but you will lose your heart to a fair and wonderful country!

What to Take With You and Why

Going into the Canoe Country without a fishing rod would be like going on your honeymoon without your new spouse. It might still be enjoyable, but not nearly so. Yet every year I see people on the portages, tramping by under their bug nets, with no rod in sight. Some may choose to forgo fishing because of a sincere lack of interest. Therapy can help these sad folks. Others may not know what to bring or be unsure of how, when or where to fish the wilderness. They should buy this book.

I will admit that when this book came out, now over two decades ago, I got a few angry letters (that was pre-email!) from folks who thought that I was being overly hard on those who had no interest in fishing. Maybe I was. It struck me as interesting, though, that apparently those who had no interest in fishing were reading a fishing book or they'd have no idea that I'd penned those words. Oh well. I learned long ago that there are plenty of critics in this world.

If you ARE interested in learning to fish the canoe country, you'll find that fishing these beautiful northwoods lakes does not require a large investment in equipment. If you are an absolute novice, this book will give you all the information you'll need to catch fish. If you are an experienced angler, and fish for the same or similar fish at home, chances are you already have most of the stuff you'll need. The trick for you is to learn what to haul along, what you must have, especially if you are unfamiliar with this area. There are no bait shops in the interior. What is in your pack when you enter will have to serve throughout the trip.

It pays then, to give your tackle needs some serious consideration before you leave home. A little homework can save you consternation in the field. Invariably you will find that you could have used a few more of this and a lot less of that. Remember, you are not fishing from a bass boat

with three tackle boxes at your feet. You must select your tackle carefully. In the Canoe Country, lugging a bunch of unnecessary items can be a very real pain in the back.

Your equipment should be easily packed and relatively light in weight. It has been said that if your tackle box has handles, you have too much stuff. Ideally your equipment, except for your rod, should fit in your pack. This leaves your hands free on the portages for swatting mosquitoes. Weight and space are never more important than when you are on a canoe trip or backpacking.

The first item to consider is your rod. Just about any style will do. If you prefer a casting rod to spinning, that's fine. Just make sure you are familiar and comfortable with it. I have found from experience and by interviewing others that the most popular rod for this wilderness is a 6 1/2 to 7 foot, medium action spinning rod. With it, of course, would go a light to medium action spinning reel.

Your rod can be carried in a rod case or exposed. There are advantages to both and each traveler must decide which way he prefers.

A rod case will protect the rod from damage both in the canoe and on portages. This can be important because a broken fishing rod in the middle of your trip can make any further fishing difficult if not impossible. The single disadvantage is that, given human nature, one is less likely to keep the rod ready to fish as you pass through lakes from one portage to the next. Many fish have been caught by trolling a lure behind the canoe as you travel. And although this is an unscientific approach, remember that you can't catch fish unless your lure is in the water.

Some who like to keep their rod out of a case prefer a slightly shorter rod, say about 5 1/2 to 6 feet, but still of a medium action. They feel the shorter rod is easier to handle on portages and takes less room in the canoe while still being ready for action. Longer rods can be broken down into two pieces while still strung, being careful not to tangle or nick the line, and the two halves bound together with a rubber band or two. This is my preferred method.

Having said that, since this book first appeared, rod manufacturers have seriously cut back on the number of models of two-piece rods. I frankly can't figure why, except perhaps that it is cheaper to make one-piece rods. If you can find a nice two-piece rod, I'd certainly recommend one – it will be easier to carry both in the canoe and on portages.

In any event, the rod is simply carried, ready to fish, across the portage or is stuck up in the bow of the canoe. The same can be done to rods in cases, or either can be taped or bound to the thwarts. You've probably noted in several of the photos in this book that we use a wood and canvas canoe. These have slotted gunwales, which allows me to use Velcro straps to bind the rods tightly below the gunwale, which provides a bit of protection. Few of you will have a canoe with such gunwales, but many canoes have gunwales that do have an amount of overhang to the inside. A little creative tinkering on your part may lead to a way to lash the rods as I do. It tends to keep them out of the way when loading and unloading packs, yet they are within easy reach for taking a quick cast.

I usually leave the rods lashed to the gunwales (or thwarts) on portages. Remember to keep the weight of anything attached to the canoe in equal balance side to side and front to back. This will make the canoe much easier to portage.

If you do carry your rods on portages, make sure you remove any lures from the rod before reaching the landing! If you've not had to remove a hook from someone, count yourself fortunate. If you've had to do it in the middle of nowhere, then you'll understand my advice. They aren't called hooks for no reason, and even if you don't snag yourself or a partner, there's a good chance that the lure will grab a pack, a lifejacket, or branches along the trail. It is just good sense to remove the lure, or wrap it in one of those heavy nylon, Velcro-closing lure bags.

Although some folks like the four and five piece pack rods, I wouldn't recommend them. The little pack rods are very nice as far as space saving goes but require even more time to put together and take apart. Being a basically lazy person I have found that pack rods greatly inhibit the prospects of my taking a cast or two into fishy looking cover as we travel through. When it is windy or the bugs are really bad the last thing you want to be doing is fiddling around trying to assemble such a rod.

My personal choice is a two piece, seven foot medium action spinning rod. I keep it strung, but broken down, the two halves held together with a couple of rubber bands. When I know we'll be traveling with no time for fishing, the rods are lashed parallel to the gunwales using Velcro straps (the kind used to bind skis together work great). Be careful when placing, or removing, packs from the canoe so you don't snag on the rods or break them. The handles on many spinning reels will fold down – another good idea to keep from breaking or bending them. I tend to lash the rods in the compartment directly in front of me. Should we decide we do have time to fish for awhile, it is a simple matter to reach forward and free the rods.

While I have never broken a rod while in the Boundary Waters, I have flattened a few guides and put some nice nicks in the rod itself. Not that I recommend using a cheap rod. These seldom hold up under the best of conditions let alone a trip into a wilderness area. Just make sure you take a sturdy rod in sound shape. If you feel uncomfortable using your best rod, take along your older, but still in good shape backup rod.

GOOD GEAR

-- Six or seven foot, light to medium action rod.

-- Matching reel, spooled with six to ten pound line.

-- Fillet knife, knife sharpener, cord stringer, needle-nosed pliers.

-- Optional: portable fish locator.

The reel should likewise be functional and should be matched to the rod. By this I mean a spinning reel on a spinning rod and a medium duty reel for a medium duty rod. Make sure the reel is working properly. Go over it, tightening the screws and giving it a few drops of oil, if needed. Now is the time to find any problems and take care of them. A loose bail spring that just sunk out of sight in Little Saganaga Lake can cause a similar reaction in your chest.

The reel should be spooled with six to ten pound monofilament line. I still prefer monofilament over the newer braided "super lines" because I actually prefer a bit of stretch, and the braided lines require a use of a monofilament leader anyway, which is one more thing to fuss with. You can, however, get away with a much stronger tensile strength line when using these extremely fine diameter braided lines, and should you be considering tangling with some very large northern pike, you may want to choose them. Deep water jigging in midsummer for lake trout is another case where the braided lines may be preferable.

For versatility, though, monofilament is still my choice. I rarely spool anything over six pounds on my reel. Your experience as a fisherman will determine how light a line you should use. The lighter the line the easier it will cast and with greater distance. It will also be less visible to the fish. There are very few fish that can't be landed on six pound line. If you have little fishing experience, go with eight or ten pound line. You will have more confidence while fighting fish and will lose fewer lures to snags.

Your line should be new and of a premium brand. If you use a spinning reel, you can take along a spare spool already wound with line. If you like, take along a refill spool of line as it comes packaged from the store.

This little watchband fish locator, with floating transducer designed to be cast, has been adapted to canoe use. A suction cup, a length of coat-hanger wire, and a bead-chain sinker, allows the transducer to stick to the side of the canoe. The sinker keeps the transducer from skipping in the water while trolling..

This will allow you to wind it on your reel or anyone else's should the need arise. A one hundred to two hundred yard spool should be more than enough. You might want to include a small leader spool for making bait rigs or you can use the line from your reel. The best bet is to make these up at home and have them ready to go. In any case, the line for these bait rigs need not be any heavier than what is on your reel, though you may want it lighter should the water be clear and the fish finicky.

To the great delight of fishing equipment manufacturers, anglers love all kinds of gadgets designed for their sport. Many of these toys are unnecessary and should be left at home. When I first wrote this book in the mid-1980s, I recommended against taking an electronic fish locator. Back in those days, these tools were large, heavy, and had very poor battery life. It is interesting to note that Quetico officials are discouraging the use of electronic fish finders (though at the time of this writing, they have not banned them) because they fear that these devices lead to increased harvest rates. I have, however, changed my mind since the first edition and find a portable locator a very nice addition -- it isn't a necessity, but nice to have.

Several very nice, truly portable fish finders have come and gone. A company called Sitex once made a nice little LCD unit that ran on AA batteries, but they discontinued it. Vexilar made, for several years, an AA battery operated fish finder (the LC-10) actually named the Boundary Waters, which, if you can find one, is excellent for use in the Canoe Country. Unfortunately, it also has been discontinued.

Because manufacturers change things, and books stay in print a long time, I hesitate to name any brands or models. As I write this in 2008, several small fish finder units are currently available. Your best bet is to do an internet search under "portable fish finders." Look for models that work on AA size batteries, as these will be the most compact. You do not need the most sophisticated locator on the market – what you want is one that will show bottom contours, depth, and give you an idea if the bottom is hard or soft. Anything beyond that is a bonus.

A recent visit to a sporting goods store revealed a couple of units that are about the size of a GPS, run on AA batteries, and have an LCD screen about the size of the one on your cell phone. They looked promising. Another manufacturer has an extremely small unit that you wear like a watch, and which has a wireless connection to a floating transducer. I've used these and they work quite well. Though the transducer is actually designed to attach to your line and float over your fishing spot, I attach mine to the side of the canoe with a suction cup and length of coat hanger wire, connecting the transducer to the wire with a 1/4 ounce bead chain sinker. The sinker helps to keep the floating transducer from skipping around on the surface when used while trolling.

Several manufacturers make LCD fish finders for boats that are reasonably small. The problem is the power supply – they are designed to feed off a boat's twelve volt system. A friend of mine went to an electronics shop and bought a small battery box for just a few dollars that allows you to place eight AA batteries in-line to produce the needed twelve volts. With a hunk of wire and a plug that matched the power port on his fish finder, he was able to power his fish locator. It works quite well, although battery time is fairly short. You may want to give it a try, though, if you already own a locator since he claims he had invested only about ten dollars in parts to build it.

Many fish locator manufacturers make battery packs and cases so that these boat-based systems can be used for ice fishing. This does make them portable, but frankly, I still think they're too bulky and heavy for a canoe trip. If you're just going in a lake or two, and then base camping, though, such a system may be just fine. There is no question, though, that a fish finder will make you a more successful angler. Whether or not you choose to haul one along is up to you.

Lake maps are an option, where available. Typically maps are only available for a few of the larger, peripheral Boundary Waters lakes. The underwater topographical features are useful for finding points and drop-offs. Some of the canoe route maps show bottom contours on a few lakes, and that's better than nothing -- though not by much. For those venturing into the Quetico, you'll find your options even more limited. Few Quetico lakes have been surveyed and so you'll find little contour information on maps. You are on your own when exploring these remote jewels. If your canoe trip revolves solely around fishing, the addition of a portable fish locator will be worth your effort.

There are some things that should be considered "must haves" for your trip. Both a fillet knife and a pocket knife should be on hand. The fillet knife, of course, is for cleaning and filleting your fish. It should have a flexible blade of six inches or more in length. Since fillet knives need to be razor sharp to do a proper job, and since they do dull easily, some means of sharpening the knife should be included in your kit. A small steel, mini-crock sticks or a small whetstone will do. The whetstone will also allow you to keep your hooks sharp. A fillet knife should be sharpened about every other fish, any longer between sharpenings will leave you with a blunted edge that will make sharpening very difficult.

The pocket knife, besides the uses you will find for it around camp, is handy while fishing to trim the ends from knots or cutting out snarls. While you could use your fillet knife for this, it dulls it needlessly and the long blade can be unwieldy for smaller tasks. Make sure both knives are as sharp as possible before leaving home; it will keep your sharpening time to a minimum in the field.

A few other tools should be taken along as well. A tiny tape measure will come in handy for making sure your fish is of a legal length to keep, as there are a few size restrictions. A needle nose pliers is a must for removing hooks from toothy mouths. They will save you countless cuts to your fingers and more importantly, allow you to quickly release uninjured and unwanted fish to the water. A lot of people don't bother to take along a landing net, myself included. They have a nasty habit of getting caught on everything while portaging, and since you will be releasing many of your fish (you can only eat so many and there is no way to keep them for days), it is a simple matter to grasp the hook with the pliers and twist it free, all while the water supports the fish.

For those fish you wish to keep, a stringer of some type will be needed. The long cord type stringers are the easiest and most foolproof of all. Simple to use, they seldom break and often find themselves doing double duty as a handy hunk of rope. The long ones, six feet or more, allow the fish to stay in deeper, cooler water. This is helpful in keeping them from going belly up on hot days. They are also nice for tying to a bush or tree on shore and still making it possible for the fish to get into deeper water. This is important if you plan on trying to keep a few fish alive for tomorrow's breakfast. I find that the braided cord stringers kink a whole lot less than the ones that are twisted.

Never cram a lot of fish on one stringer if you plan on keeping them alive for any amount of time. If you do try to keep them overnight, I have found that two or three fish are about the maximum on one stringer. Cord stringers are light, cheap and last indefinitely so you might want to consider throwing a couple in the pack. It is nice to have one at each end of the canoe so you don't have to toss fish from one end to the other.

Other possible niceties would include a hook hone, a de-liar scale for the curious or honest, some parachute cord to use as anchor rope and, if you want to keep some fish for home, a burlap sack.

Portage anchors can be made by using a nylon stuff-sack filled with rocks (much easier than trying to tie a line to a rock!). They'll get banged up and torn eventually, but are very useful on windy days. These handy

anchors weigh almost nothing until filled with rocks and roll up to be quite small. It makes the task of locating an anchor a simple one because if there is one thing the Canoe Country has plenty of, it is rocks. You should not underestimate the importance of an anchor for fishing. I use a hunk of parachute cord as anchor line. Roll the cord up and put it in the stuff-sack when not in use.

The burlap sack is for keeping fish fresh and cool. Placing fish in a thoroughly soaked bag will maintain a steady temperature; cool enough to keep them fresh for a day. This should be enough time to get them to the next camp or back to the car. Nothing more than a variation of the old desert water bag trick, just make sure you keep the sack up in the shade, keep it damp, and keep it where it is exposed to the air so that the evaporation process can work. Burlap sacks aren't as easy to find as they once were, but a visit to the produce manager at your local grocery store should yield one -- potatoes are still often delivered in these sacks.

Your tackle needs will be based on what species of fish you are after and to a certain extent, how serious you are. Some individuals will be willing to carry a bit more than others. But keep in mind that this is one case where more is not always better. A lot of tackle is interchangeable from one species to the next. A smaller portion is more specific in nature. Of course, if your trip is centered on just one species, your tackle can be tailored for it.

We will get into specific needs in the chapters on each fish species. The following list of tackle is a suggestion based upon the premise that you want to try for all of major Canoe Country species. All of the tackle listed are tried and true favorites of the area, and while you may not see some of your favorites on the list, a tackle box filled with these or similar ingredients will see you through very nicely.

- hooks, bait type, with short shank in sizes 6 or 4. Bring plenty. **(Note: Quetico has banned live bait)**.
- sinkers, split shot, slip sinkers and a few bead-chain keel sinkers for trolling. Bring a range of split shot, 1/8 to 1/2 ounce in the slip and keel sinkers. For deep water trolling during midsummer you can link several sinkers together. Use nontoxic sinkers, if possible. It is only a matter of time until lead will be banned in the Canoe Country anyway.
- swivels, snap type, and duo-lock type non-swivel snaps.
- plastic bodied jigs, 1/8 to 3/8 ounce, with and without spinner blades. Best colors are chartreuse, yellow, black, brown and purple. Bring extra bodies.
- plugs (crankbaits, stickbaits), both surface and diving. Trolling plugs can be 2 to 5 inches in length, surface plugs for smallmouth should be no longer than 1 1/2 to 2 inches. Colors best in silver, gold, blue, orange and perch.
- spinners, such as the Mepps and Vibrax in sizes 1 and 2. Silver or gold blades and with or without squirrel tails.
- spoons, both heavy for casting (1/2 to 7/8 ounce) and lightweight for trolling ("flutter spoons"). Both types in silver, gold, hammered brass, gold/orange and red/white. For deep water vertical jigging for lake trout, some 1/2 and 1 ounce Heddon Sonars.

- a couple of bobbers, slip type preferably, if bait fishing.
- poppers, both hair and cork, for the fly fisherman. Best sizes for smallmouth are 8, 6, and 4. Some streamers and a few dry flies.

Please note that Quetico has banned barbed hooks. Currently you can just flatten the barbs of a regular hook with your pliers and be in compliance. You can have barbed hooks in your tackle box, but not on your line. But, because rules change, it would be wise for you to check the rules before venturing into the park. It is possible that Canadian officials will, at some point, require truly barbless hooks for all fishing. You've been warned!

At first glance this may sound like a lot of tackle but once assembled you should find that it will pack quite small and portageable. When concentrating on one type of fishing on a trip you can beef up that area of tackle, and eliminate others.

All of your tackle except the pliers, stringer and the fillet knife, should fit into one small box. Some anglers, myself included, prefer those flat tackle boxes that are about the size of a cigar box – my box is about six by nine inches, and an inch or so deep. Each angler should have their own box so that you're not passing things back and forth in the canoe. Find it hard to believe you can get all you need into a box of that size? I've gone on canoe trips weeks in length and never run short of tackle even though this small box was all that I was carrying. Frankly, if you have need of more space than this you probably have too much stuff.

A box like this will sit nicely under the top flap of a Duluth pack, no matter how stuffed it already is. You want to keep the tackle, as well as the rod, accessible so that you won't hesitate to take a few casts as you paddle along.

What about live bait? Well, it is a fact that live bait can improve your fishing success. At times, when the fish are finicky, live bait may be the only thing that will work. That doesn't mean you must have it. If all you have are artificial lures and you know how to use them, you'll catch fish. But bait will give you an advantage.

SPECIAL QUETICO REGULATIONS:

*-- BARBLESS HOOKS ARE REQUIRED; IT IS **OK** TO MASH DOWN BARBED HOOKS.*

-- NO "ORGANIC" BAIT; THAT MEANS NO LIVE OR PRESERVED BAIT (MINNOWS, LEECHES, WORMS, OR FISH EGGS).

-- SIZE RESTRICTIONS ON SOME SPECIES ARE IN PLACE; BRING A TAPE MEASURE.

Having said that, you need to know that the use of live bait – indeed "organic bait" – has been banned in Quetico Provincial Park. Organic bait would include preserved (salted, freeze dried, etc.) minnows, leeches, fish eggs, and the like. This isn't solely a ban on bringing bait into the park, but a ban on USING bait. This is important because some anglers believe they can trap live bait while in the park. Nope. You can not use live (or once alive) bait at all in the Quetico.

Rules are different in the Boundary Waters, and I don't foresee a ban on live bait any time soon. However, it is always wise to check the rules before entering. The following live bait advice then applies only to those going into the Boundary Waters.

Live bait does not always travel well and it is always an added nuisance. Only you can decide if it is worth your time and effort. However, there are baits that travel better than others and there are also frozen, salted and freeze dried baits. The preserved baits can take the place of live baits when they are used for bottom fishing or tipping an artificial lure.

The two live baits that get the nod for ease in transporting and care are leeches and worms. These are primarily bass and walleye baits. Both are easy to carry, even in large numbers, and are simple to care for. They are also pretty much interchangeable although fish can show a preference toward one on certain days or seasons. Generally, fish will take leeches better during the spring than they will worms.

The major enemy of both baits is heat. If you can keep them cool, and change the leech's water frequently, you'll be able to keep them squirming throughout your trip. A small cooler, six pack size, is perfect for this. The new soft-sided coolers are nice, because once the bait is gone, you can flatten it and bury it in a pack. Put the leeches into a sturdy plastic bag before putting them in the cooler and seal the bag with a twist-tie or rubber band. This will allow you to set the cooler in the pack without leaking on the macaroni and cheese. I usually put the bait cooler in the food pack because bait smells edible – to bears, that is. Best to keep everything that might attract bears in one pack. If you have it available, throw a little ice on the bait at the beginning of the trip. Any amount of cooling you can do to the leeches or worms at the start will just extend their life that much further into the trip. Whether in camp or canoe, keep the bait in the shade as nothing will cook them faster than the sun.

I've found that a wide-mouth, plastic water bottle is a handy container for transporting leeches. They are tough and leakproof. Once used for this purpose, though, you had better label it so you can tell it apart from your other bottles. Lemonade mixed in one of these bottles has a very distinctive flavor.

Minnows are another matter entirely. They require frequent changes of water and also must be kept cool. Minnow buckets are large and cumbersome, have a tendency to spill and splash, and are a general nuisance on portages. Those of you planning on covering a lot of territory will soon decide that minnows are not worth the effort.

If you are going to be setting up a base camp and traveling from there, taking minnows is less of a problem. Have the bait dealer put your minnows in an oxygen pack. An oxygen pack is nothing more than a very heavy plastic bag into which the minnows and a small amount of water are placed. It is then pumped full of pure oxygen and sealed with a rubber band. Packed like this, and kept cool and unopened, the minnows will keep for up to three or four days. This gives you enough time to reach a base camp after which the minnows can be put into a minnow bucket and submerged in the lake. Another twist is to have minnows put in multiple oxygen packs, each filled with a day or two's worth of minnows, only opening the packs, one at a time, as you need them.

If live minnows are not a necessity, an alternative would be to take freeze-dried or salted minnows. These keep indefinitely and are more than adequate for bottom fishing for lake trout and northern. They also work well for trolling or for tipping a spoon or jig since this normally requires hooking a minnow through the head, a process that kills the bait anyway.

The best all around live minnow to take is the fathead chub. They are hardy and available in a range of sizes. Chubs work well on just about any species of fish that you may be after. Sucker minnows are also a good bet and the large sizes are the preferred bait for big northerns and lake trout. When using preserved bait try shiner minnows or smelt. Shiners are just about impossible to keep alive anyway but are very effective bait. Smelt are generally not available in any other form. Both are deadly on lake trout and northerns.

Whatever bait you choose to use, remember these points. Live or preserved bait can increase your fishing success. All live bait must be kept cool and some require frequent changes in water. Try to put them in sturdy containers and if possible, try to fit them in your pack in order to keep hassles along the portages to a minimum. Never release your live bait into the water (minnows or leeches) or worms on land. Earthworms are not native to the Canoe Country and can alter the soil of the forest floor to the point that certain native plants can't survive. Introducing a new species of minnow or leech to a wilderness lake is also a really poor idea. And don't take any kind of live or preserved baits into the Quetico!

Is there a good alternative to live bait that performs better than plastic or metal lures? Yes.

In recent years, tackle manufactures have developed artificial leeches, minnows, worms and all manner of creepy crawly lures for use on jigs or other rigs out of substances that smell good to fish, and are biodegradable. One such brand currently available, and which I've used with great success, is Berkley Gulp. I won't go quite as far as saying that it performs as well as live bait, but honestly, it works nearly as well. I find it no hardship to leave the leeches and worms behind when I have this stuff in my pack. Not only does it perform admirably, but it saves the hassle of trying to keep bait alive. Give it a try.

Just remember to keep your fishing gear to a minimum in size and weight. Pack it well so that it doesn't scatter all over the place in the bottom of the canoe or on portages. While it is tempting to haul a lot of gear, my decades of experience show that you actually will use less tackle than you think. The most important things to stock up on are extra jigs and bodies for them.

Regardless of what types of baits and lures you take remember to give it a little thought and consideration. Check that rod and reel over and then get ready. You're about to head into some of the finest fishing country God ever laid his hand to.

Wilderness Walleyes

The most sought after fish in Minnesota, the walleye is equally popular within the Boundary Waters. The largest member of the perch family, it is not pursued because of any legendary fighting prowess. The most fighting involved with walleyes is who is going to get the last fillet from the frying pan. For this is the real basis of the walleye's popularity, it is delectable dinner fare.

Not that some aren't respectable on the end of a rod. It's just that they aren't very memorable either. Many a big walleye has been mistaken for a snag being retrieved from the bottom, much to the surprise of the fisherman when he sees those big, luminous eyes coming up toward him.

I suspect that the rest of their popularity comes from the fact that the average walleye, around a couple of pounds, is fairly easy to catch. True, there are times during the year when catching walleyes can be a downright mystery, but for the most part they are fairly predictable. Consistently catching above average size walleyes is another matter entirely.

This receives a lot of attention by those "pro" anglers and they often raise a lot of hullabaloo while trying to make a science of walleye fishing. You have your backtrolling, oxygen meters, temperature gauges and video sonar. You have your "hawg" walleyes, structure, weedlines and the rest of the terminology. Of course, you have a bass boat with two outboard motors and an electric trolling motor, all of this to catch a meal of walleyes and most of which means diddly-squat for the wilderness canoeing angler.

The truth of the matter is that with a little common sense, the ability to read water, maybe a topographic map of the lake or a portable fish locator, and some basic background on the likes, dislikes and habits of walleyes, you can do a respectable job of catching your dinner.

The real reason walleyes are so popular!

Many of the lakes in the BWCAW and Quetico are crawling with walleyes. There are lots of large walleyes up there and the Minnesota state record fish came from the Seagull River where it enters Saganaga Lake. This monster weighed in at 17 pounds, 8 ounces. Each year many fish are taken in the ten pound range. Any walleye over six pounds is a big fish and the "keeper" fish start at about a pound and a half.

According to the Minnesota Department of Natural Resources, the walleye is the most sought-after fish in Minnesota. Its thick, white fillets, handsome shape and coloring, and elusive nature make it the ultimate prize among anglers. Each year, anglers in Minnesota keep roughly three and a half million walleyes totaling four million pounds. The average walleye caught and kept is about fourteen inches long and weighs slightly more than one pound. The walleye is named for its pearlescent eye, which is caused by a reflective layer of pigment, called the tapetum lucidum, that helps it see and feed at night or in murky water.

A close cousin of the walleye is the sauger. Sauger have a more limited distribution than walleyes, and they don't grow as large. The two species look similar, but you can tell them apart by looking at the tip of the lower part of the tail. That part of the tail is white on a walleye, but not on a sauger. You won't find many sauger in the Canoe Country. Most, if not all, of the lakes that contain sauger are found in the Quetico.

Big walleyes can be taken in the Canoe Country, even if you don't know what you are doing! I'm proof of that. My father hauled me into the outback one June for a little walleye fishing. We were joined by my brother Butch, who was a popular fishing guide in the area at that time and a buddy of his who was also taking money for fishing under the poor pretense of doing it for a living.

We were on one of those large border lakes, Butch selecting the lake because of its reputation for nice fish, and we had lashed the two canoes together with popple poles making a veritable catamaran. They told me that this was for greater stability on the large water but I now suspect it may have been because, at eight years old, I was not much help in handling a canoe. Butch and I were in the one canoe, my dad and the other guide in the second.

Two things stand out in my mind about that day. One was the fact that the mosquitoes were large and plentiful. "So big," my father said, "that they had woodticks on them." The other memory centered around my brand new fishing rod that my father had proudly produced after work the night before we left. It was one of those new fangled fiberglass jobs with a push button spincasting reel. My previous rod had been made of steel. The reel came all loaded with monofilament line that must have been about one hundred pound test. With the solid glass rod and the heavy line I could cast about thirty feet. There was no way I could hang a lure in the trees along shore with that rig, a thought that may have crossed my father's mind when he selected it. In any case, I thought it was beautiful.

We were trolling along with a new secret lure Butch had discovered. It was a balsa wood minnow, silver in color and about four inches long, straight from Finland. Later, someone was to make a couple of zillion dollars marketing these things under the name of Rapala. True to the form of serious fishermen (or dense) we were not concerned with how much money the lure might make for someone, we just knew they caught fish. The lure was called a Talus.

As the innumerable spruce trees slid past the slow moving canoes, each one harboring equally uncountable mosquitoes, my rod doubled over. I yanked on that thing as hard as I could, only to feel it stop dead. "Fish?" asked Butch. "Naw, only a snag," I returned. To my chagrin the line started to cut through the water away from the canoe. It was, indeed, a fish. The battle on, it soon became obvious that this was not just a fish, but a large one. After a couple of minutes of my reeling against the drag, the rod tip under the canoe and my relentless pumping of the rod, my father, in the next canoe if you remember, told my brother to take the rod away from me. The fish was too big for me to handle. I didn't know any swear words at that age, but if I had, I'm sure I would have used a few choice ones at that point, father or no father.

To my undying gratitude Butch said, "No, let him handle it, he's got to learn to fight his own big fish."

With the heavy monofilament line, the stiff glass rod, and two sets of treble hooks, my father needn't have worried. I think I cranked that walleye right up to the top guide of the doubled over rod. Butch told me to work it back toward him and with his help, like a derrick, I swung that fish through the air into the canoe. This fish just was destined to be mine.

Flopping around in the bottom of the canoe, the fish was only surpassed in size by the roundness of my eyes. On the stringer finally, Butch passed it up to me to inspect. I tied that stringer to the canoe seat with about twelve knots, and lowered him over the side. I really don't remember much about what the rest of the party was doing at that point or for the rest of the day. I spent the next five hours or so bent over the canoe, watching my fish, making sure it didn't get away. When we weighed it later that day it neared nine pounds. Despite all the things that could have gone wrong, this old moss backed, marble eyed monster was mine.

And if an eight year old can do it, so can you.

Walleyes, also known as *Stizostedian vitreum vitreum*, prefer larger bodies of water. They are identified by their light colored belly, olive green or brassy sides, six or seven dark bands crossing their back and a milk white tip to the bottom of their tail. However, some Canoe Country lakes contain walleyes that are almost black on the sides, possibly the result of isolated genetics, living in deep, dark water or the combination of both. Mary Jo and I have found a few places in the Quetico where the walleyes have a very distinctive blue coloration. In any case, you can't miss those marble sized, pale glowing eyes for which the fish are named.

These big eyes can tell us something important. Walleyes are very light sensitive. They feed primarily at dawn and dusk and bright, calm days are usually poor for fishing. Overcast days with a slight chop on the water to cut down the light penetration will invariably help your walleye fishing. It even goes to the extreme that walleyes will be found on the shady side of reefs and can go up or down the reef with the angle and penetration of the sun.

Walleyes are even night spawners. They spawn in the spring, just after ice-out, and the dates for this event fluctuate with the weather of that particular year. In the Canoe Country, spawning occurs just before the Minnesota general fishing opener.

Walleyes spawn in rivers or on lake shoals where there is wind and wave action. When they spawn they will be highly concentrated. They are also very susceptible to a lure at this time and the combination of both sometimes forces the DNR to close areas to fishing in order to allow the fish to spawn unmolested. Most of the spawning will occur when the water temperature reaches 45 to 50 degrees. At this time of year many big fish are landed and these are almost always females, the males being much smaller.

It often happens that the walleye spawning has just ended when the fishing season opens. The opener is the first trip of the year for many wanderers in the Canoe Country. This can be a very fruitless experience because the fishing for walleyes immediately after they have spawned is almost the worst of the year. It seems that they feed very little during this time and are also quite scattered as they move back to their traditional summer haunts. When this occurs I recommend that you go lake trout fishing. It is at its best at this time.

Now the "pros" term this the "post-spawn period" and have tried to figure out all kinds of things you can do in order to catch walleyes at this time. I still recommend that you go lake trout fishing. But if you insist on fishing for walleyes when they aren't feeding, you can try a couple of things.

Walleyes like warm water and chances are you will have your best luck by looking for them in parts of the lake that warm up more quickly than the rest, i.e., shallow bays and shores. Even this warmer water is likely to be below their preferred temperature, so fish slowly. Walleyes are methodical, deliberate feeders and when the water is cold they will be even slower. These shallow bays are sometimes very muddy bottomed, generally a no-no in walleye fishing since they like hard bottoms. There may well be, however, some gravel or a rock pile amidst that warm muddy bay. That is where the walleyes would be. They also like to feed on insect larvae during the early part of the season and these are hatched in areas like this. With a rock pile near by to home in on, they can make feeding forays into the insect laden areas.

Tips For Walleyes

-- ALWAYS ASK A LOCAL BAIT SHOP THE DEPTH AT WHICH WALLEYES ARE CURRENTLY BEING TAKEN.

-- WALLEYES HAVE GREAT SIGHT; USE LIGHT LINE.

-- WALLEYES ARE ALMOST ALWAYS RIGHT ON THE BOTTOM; IF YOU'RE NOT TOUCHING BOTTOM WITH YOUR LURE, YOU WON'T CATCH WALLEYES!

Walleye fishing is at its best when this slow period ends and they have again set up shop for the summer on their favorite reef or shoal. These prime locations are characteristic in nature. They generally have abrupt changes in their topography, are near deep water and are rocky. Stay away from mucky bottoms; walleyes like hard bottoms, be they sand, gravel or rubble.

During the first month in which the walleyes have returned to their summer haunts, the fish will be in fairly shallow water. By shallow I mean in the range of five to fifteen feet. The factors that will influence at exactly what depth the fish will be found should be carefully examined when you begin fishing. These factors include water clarity, temperature, amount of sunlight and direction and strength of the wind. The time of day can also affect the fish's behavior. It is always wise – I consider it a must – to stop by a bait shop near the edge of the wilderness, buy a couple of lures, and talk to the people who work there. In particular, you want to ask at what depth the locals have been finding the walleyes. It makes no difference if the lakes they've been fishing are inside, or outside, the wilderness. Knowing that the fish are being consistently found at a particular depth can save you hours, even days, of searching on your own.

Remember walleyes are very light conscious. A bright day on a very clear lake will likely mean fairly deep fish, even early in the season. The same day and lake, with a slight chop to the water will probably bring the fish up. During the same bright day, with or without a wind, the morning and evening are bound to be better times to be fishing. Unless you're a real diehard you might as well put up the hammock and read a book during the middle of bright, calm days.

To be on the safe side during your early summer, late spring fishing trips, start looking for walleyes in about five feet of water. Unless the day is extremely dark, the water exceptionally murky or its temperature very cold, the fish are not likely to be shallower than that. However, their habits are not always predictable and there are times when they could be right up next to shore, so be flexible.

At any time of year you will want to look for walleyes over rocky reefs, shoals and points. These types of structures are pretty easy to spot just by examining the lake's shoreline. Watch for rubble beaches and points and then examine the water off these. You want to determine if this same type of rocky nature is carried out into the lake. If there is a topographic map of your lake available it can save you some time by directing you to likely looking areas. If you have a portable fish locator, now is the time to break it out. Look for drop-offs or any other irregularities that show up at the walleye's preferred depths.

Even the best fish locators often don't show walleyes very well, as these fish often hug the very bottom. The locator's main purpose is to find the structure – drop-offs, rubble mounds, etc. – around which the fish like to live.

Walleyes feed on the bottom and are schooling fish, two points that are in the fisherman's favor. Except at certain odd times of the year when walleyes will suspend far off the bottom in order to find the right combination of water temperature and oxygen, they will be right down among the rocks. Once you find one down there, chances are you'll find more.

The most popular method for locating fish is by trolling. In the Canoe Country this means a lot of paddling. By trolling you can cover a lot of water in a relatively short amount of time. If you do locate fish -- that is, you catch one -- mark the spot immediately. This can be done with a small buoy or by making visual triangulations with landmarks on shore. You could also ease out the anchor. It is important to quickly mark the spot because of the walleye's schooling habit. Too many fishermen consider the happy chance of catching a fish just that, a chance, and then continue blissfully on their way. Mark that spot!

When trolling, the very best lures are minnow imitating plugs like the original floating Rapala. These plugs should be about three to four inches in length and the best colors are silver, gold or perch-like finishes. I've found that floating plugs have better action than the sinking models and would advise using a floater with a sinker, if necessary, over the sinking models. A small bead chain swivel sinker three feet or so from the lure works best and helps to keep line twist to a minimum. In a pinch, split shot can be used.

So why use a floating plug and a sinker if you're tying to fish ten feet down? As mentioned, the floating plugs have, I'm convinced, a more realistic swimming motion. But more important than that, you'll hang up

(get snagged on the bottom) far less often. These lures will have two sets of treble hooks, one at the middle and one at the tail. I ALWAYS remove the front treble hook set. With a sinker two or three feet up the line, the lure will swim slightly nose-down. By removing these front hooks, you'll eliminate most bottom hang-ups. The sinker is the part of your rig that is bouncing along the bottom, and sinkers don't get hung up easily! And when they do, it is usually a simple matter of back paddling over the spot where it is hung up and pulling from the opposite direction to get it to release.

Won't removing the front hooks decrease your chances of catching fish? I don't believe so. Experience has proved to me that fish are almost always hooked by the rear-most hooks, and the front hooks tend to catch on the fish's head, eyes, or in your thumb. Getting rid of the front hooks saves both you and the fish some pain, reduces hang-ups, and makes releasing fish much, much easier.

A slow trolling speed for walleyes is important. Most anglers troll too quickly and this results in far fewer strikes. On a day with little or no wind, one person paddling slowly is about the right speed. If wind makes it necessary for both to paddle, keep it as slow as you can while still being able to maintain control of the canoe. If it is windy enough, and the wind is blowing in the right direction, try using the wind as your trolling motor. This can be very effective. If the wind pushes you along too quickly, ease one paddle over the side, and place its blade at a ninety-degree angle to the canoe. It will act like a brake.

Try to troll parallel to reefs and points. One pass is not always enough if the cover looks good. You may have to experiment a little with the depth and speed, which may seem time consuming. In the long run, though, enticing fish near you to strike is a lot quicker than chasing greener pastures, especially when you have to paddle to get to them. If the structure is right, there should be fish on it somewhere, and patience will win out.

Because paddling for endless hours can be wearing, take the opportunity to use the wind if it presents itself. Let it drift you over likely looking areas and bounce a jig along, or if going very slowly, cast with a countdown type plug. By bouncing a jig along you kill two birds with one stone. The tick-tick-tick of the jig on the bottom can give you an idea of what the bottom looks like and how hard it is. At the same time you stand a good chance of catching a walleye. It is best to plan your drift to run parallel to the structure, or quartering it, rather than quickly up one side and down the other.

There may be times when you wish to both travel quickly and troll. For years it bothered me that, while "making time" on a travel day, we were passing over what was obviously prime fishing waters. At traveling speeds, most fishing lures do not run well even if you did toss one over the side. Most will end up spinning and tangling your line, or will simply scoot along near the surface, where they are unlikely to attract a fish. In the last few years, however, I've found a type of plug that will allow you to both travel and troll quickly.

These plugs are known as "no-bill" crankbaits. Several manufacturers make this kind of lure, and they all perform in much the same manner, but so that you have some idea what they look like, I suggest finding a Rapala Rattlin' Rap. The half ounce size seems to be the best all around and I've had my best luck on perch-like colors and the basic black/silver combination. These teardrop shaped plugs have a thin profile and will not twist or spin when pulled at high speeds. They are a sinking lure so that little weight needs to be added if you are fishing in five feet of water or less. A keel sinker four feet up the line will allow you to fish deeper waters, up to about fifteen feet, depending upon the weight of the sinker you've attached and the speed at which you're paddling.

Again, I remove the front set of treble hooks to reduce the number of snags. These plugs, and most others, run with the nose down. Since the rear hook is riding high and behind the lure, and the front treble has been removed, this type of plug can bounce bottom very frequently without hanging up.

The rare snag occurs when the lure swims into a rock pile and becomes wedged. These can usually be removed by reversing your direction. This bottom bouncing technique is critical for walleye success and is also effective on northern pike and smallmouth bass. The same lure and high speed trolling technique is also effective on spring lake trout when they are cruising over shallow reefs.

This technique is probably no one's first choice in fishing methods but, when done on those days when you'll spend most of your time traveling, will provide many bonus fish and supply some dinners. It is helpful to modify your route, if convenient, to pass near points of land, near islands or along shore to put you in likely fish habitat. You'll also need to prop your rod within reaching distance and in a manner that does not allow it to be pulled backward or overboard. These "no-bill" crankbaits put a pretty fair bend in your rod when you reach top speed and you'll also need to be prepared for the eventual strike or snag.

Don't panic if your lure bounces bottom and the rod tip swings back. Leave your drag set lightly in the event you truly hang up. Most of the time you'll find that the lure has only briefly touched bottom but not gotten snagged. Believe me, I've worn the front end clean off of many plugs without losing them to the lake bottom. By keeping the lure in close proximity of the bottom, you'll greatly increase the number of strikes you'll receive.

There is one other specialized technique I use for wilderness walleyes (and it works for bass and northerns, too).

While the fishing magazines will be filled with drawings of drop-offs, points, reefs, and other types of structure that typically hold walleyes, the fact is that many Canoe Country lakes are steep sided, with little structure. Often they are a simple gash in the Precambrian rock. They hold fish, but the fish are shore oriented, for the center of the lake is often devoid structure. And there will be times – believe me – when you might be on a lake with lots of islands and structure, but heavy winds will keep you pinned down along a lee shore, a shoreline that disappears into the depths quickly.

Now if you've read all the pro-walleye articles, you'd be convinced that the only place you could find fish in this lake would be on the reefs and around the islands, for the steep shorelines meant equally steep underwater topography, with little classic walleye structure. And if you believed so, you'd be wrong.

Walleyes along these steep shores will be in a very narrow band, suspended above or just to the side of their preferred depth. Think of the structure below as a very steep slope, falling nearly vertically away from the shallows. If you travel along the shoreline, these underwater cliffs aren't uniform. Some parts are steeper (a narrower "walleye zone") and others less so, with a broader target area. In all cases, the places where walleyes will be found will be smaller and harder to target than the classic reefs and island structures, which tend to be larger and much more defined.

MORE WALLEYE TIPS

-- CLOUDY DAYS ARE BETTER THAN BRIGHT DAYS.

-- A CHOP ON THE WATER IS BETTER THAN FLAT CALM.

-- WALLEYES ARE RARELY DEEP, WHICH MEANS THEY CAN HEAR BANGING IN THE CANOE. BE QUIET!

-- WALLEYES ARE SCHOOL-ING FISH. IF YOU FIND ONE, MARK THE SPOT. THERE WILL BE MORE!

And this is what makes fishing such areas difficult. For instance, throwing a jig toward shore means that it will likely land too shallow at the onset, then rapidly pass through the walleye zone (if at all) on the retrieve. The reason for this is that few of us are truly adept at walking a jig downhill as they are retrieving it toward themselves. It is a hard thing to do. Most of the time, the jig ends up passing over the area that walleyes might be found. For similar reasons, it is equally difficult to keep a slip bobber or slip sinker rig at the right depth along such steep shores. And even if you are really good at fishing a jig toward shore, it will pass through the walleye zone very quickly.

It is also more difficult to find the proper depth along these shore. On a reef, one might drift with a jig, testing various depths until a fish takes. Since walleyes are often tight to the bottom, even a fish locator doesn't always see them, so being able to methodically work various depths until the walleyes are found is a huge advantage.

Cliff-side walleyes aren't so easy to find because the zone is so small. A fish locator is a big help, but not for the reason you might think. It is often difficult to actually see the fish themselves, but as any serious walleye angler knows, the greatest aid these devices lend is in helping us find the depths at which walleyes might be found.

And what are those depths?

Many of these steeper Canoe Country lakes are cold. They may (and probably do) harbor not only walleyes, northern pike and perhaps smallmouth bass, but lake trout too. Given the coldness of these lakes, it is very, very rare to encounter walleyes below twenty or so feet deep, and more often than not, even into August, most walleyes will be found at ten to fifteen feet. In June, they'll be even shallower.

So how, then, does one fish these narrow shoreline walleye zones?

The answer is quite simple. Troll.

Trolling is by far the most effective means of prospecting these shores, because, by traveling parallel to shore, you can more easily keep your lure at the correct depth (provided you've found it!).

Second, you'll need to fish parallel to shore, and with a lure that can retain a constant depth. The best shoreline prospecting rig is a simple floating stick bait, such as the original floating Rapala or a floating Shad Rap, with a bead chain swivel sinker three feet or so up the line. Sinkers of different weights will put your lure at different depths, so adding or removing lead until the first fish is found is the key. The angle of your stick bait's diving lip also influences how rapidly it dives. To make changing lures or sinkers easy, use a duo-lock snap at the end of the line from your reel, and at both ends of your three foot leader. Never use a snap swivel on the end attached to the stick bait, though, for it adversely affects the lure's action. Bead chain sinkers have a built in swivel which is enough to insure your line doesn't twist.

Don't continue to drag a lure at ten feet deep all day long if nothing is going on. Move up, move down, but move! Eventually, you'll encounter that first walleye. And all other things being equal, other walleyes will be found at the same depth.

If you're rod is out at a ninety degree angle on the right side, and your partner's on the left, it is entirely possible for the two of you to be fishing at very different depths, so steep are these underwater cliffs. This can be an advantage when first scouting for the right depth. The inshore person may want to put on only a one-eighth or quarter ounce sinker, and fish down to about ten feet. The outside rod can be rigged with a three-eighths or half ounce sinker, and fished more deeply. But once the prospecting is over, and the correct depth is determined, all rods should

be rigged to the proper depth so that they can fish the same zone. This may mean having the stern paddler's rod go straight out the back of the canoe, so that the bow paddler's line can be more or less directly under the canoe, thus avoiding tangles, and keeping both at the same depth.

Don't paddle too far from shore, either. There are times we've had great walleye angling while paddling just a canoe length from the trees or a cliff, and yet our lures were nearly twenty feet down. If there is a wind, and provided it isn't too strong for safe or comfortable paddling, the shoreline that is getting the wind is often more productive than that in the lee because the wave action stirs up food.

There are a few other advantages to this technique. First, you cover more territory, increasing the odds of a strike. Second, there's a good chance you'll also pick up some nice northern pike or smallmouth while fishing the shorelines. Third, you'll see many wonderful things while paddling this close to shore, like pitcher plants, or a mink. Finally, you can often fish shorelines on days when wind would otherwise keep you from comfortably fishing, or even reaching, mid-lake reefs and islands.

Hopefully after drift fishing or trolling for a while you will have tied into a fish or two and marked the spot. Because walleyes are such slow feeders it is nearly always preferable to fish from a stationary craft. You can better control the depth of your bait, get a superior feel of the bottom and allow the fish the time to play with the bait, if using live bait.

Probably the best artificial lures for still fishing for walleyes are jigs. The best colors are yellow, chartreuse, orange, white and black in about a 1/4 ounce size. If someone forced me to go with just one color, there is no question that I'd choose chartreuse. Yellow would be an awfully close second. Some jigs come with a spinner blade above the body. These also work very well and the blade sometimes helps to attract reluctant fish.

While hair and feather bodied jigs are still available (and work well), the vast majority of jigs now have plastic bodies. I've taken to buying jigs without any bodies at all (some stores offer bulk purchases of such jigs) and then stock up on the plastic bodies in the colors I prefer. Of late, as I mentioned in the chapter on equipment, I've been using the Berkley Gulp bodies. They look like plastic bodies, but fish tend to take them more readily, even when they are finicky. By the way, once these bodies have gotten wet, they will harden to a rock-like state when exposed to air. Either remove them while they are still soft, or wrap them with a piece of plastic to keep them moist. And just because they are biodegradable, don't go tossing them into the lake once they've gotten chewed up!

If you do have live bait available it is often helpful to tip the jig with a minnow, leech or piece of worm. Sometimes this combination works when nothing else will. Since leeches and worms travel easier than do live minnows they often get the nod as the canoeist's bait. Leeches catch walleyes from opening day of the fishing season on, with the worms catching up in the summer. Minnows inflows are at their best in the spring and fall. And remember – no organic bait, alive or dead, in the Quetico!

Live bait rigs for walleyes are very simple. The best type are the "Lindy" rigs which can be purchased or made by yourself. The hook size should be small and short-shanked. A bait hook in a size six should suffice.

When using a small bait hook, the sinker should be placed about a foot and a half to three feet above. This can be a medium split shot or a slip sinker. Slip sinkers allow the fish to pick up the bait and run a distance with it, a favorite trick of walleyes, before stopping to swallow it. Because the line slips through the sinker the fish feels no resistance. In order to keep the sinker the proper distance from the hook a tiny swivel is tied in to act as a stopper. A quicker method is to use one of those teeny little split shot on the line to stop the slip sinker. Slip sinkers for walleyes should be about 1/4 to 1/8 ounce.

Another handy item for live bait fishing are floating jig heads. Floating jig heads look like jigs but keep your bait off the bottom with their cork or foam head. Many live baits will hide between rocks or in the weeds if given a chance, a habit that will reduce their visibility to the fish and your likelihood of getting strikes. Floating jig heads will keep them at the depth you determine by how far up the line your sinker is placed. The best colors for these floats are orange, chartreuse and yellow.

As the summer progresses and the temperatures rise, walleyes will go deeper, sometimes as deep as thirty to fifty feet. So must you. The techniques are the same as before but it may be a bit more difficult to locate the right structure. A good place to start are the same reefs and points you located before. Many of these will run into the deeper water you and the walleyes are seeking.

Evening and morning fishing becomes important during the hotter months because at these times the walleyes will sneak back into the shallower water, thereby giving you easier access to them. The very best time to catch walleyes then will be the first and last hours of light. Night fishing can be very productive as well. This actually works out well for many canoeists as they may wish to travel during the middle of the day or take time out for some other form of recreation.

And now a word about wind. Several years ago my wife, Mary Jo, and I were fishing Sunday Bay of Crooked lake. It was June, and the walleyes should have been shallow – ten feet deep or less. I say should have been because they weren't – or if they were, I sure couldn't buy a bite.

While I was busy in the canoe tying on yet another lure to see if I could find one that would entice a walleye to join us for dinner, Mary Jo asked me the lake depth below us. We had drifted out into some open water while I was fussing around with lures, and the fish locator revealed we were in thirty feet of water. I told her the depth, and also said not to bother fishing that deep, since the fish would never be that deep that early in the year.

Well, you know where this story is going. She didn't listen to me, but instead dropped her jig down over the side and fed out line until she was on the bottom. And of course, she immediately was fast into a nice walleye. She was positively gloating....

So why were the walleyes so deep? It had been a windy – a horribly windy – five days before we had departed on our trip. The wind had blown so hard and for so long, that the lakes had "turned over." That simply means that the wind action had stirred things up so much that the cold water had risen to the top as the warm water had been swirled under. The walleyes simply followed the warm water. Within two days, the whole process reversed itself, as the less dense warm water surfaced.

Which just goes to show you that even if you think you know what you're doing, even if you KNOW the walleyes are going to be shallow, you can be fooled by mother nature. And your wife.

The moral of the story, and all the fishing tips that preceded it, is that you need to be flexible. Multiple methods for a variety of conditions are the norm. Experiment. The fish are there, and usually, they will bite. It is a matter of methodically trying new spots, new lures, new depths and new techniques until that first walleye is found. After that, you're home free, because as schooling fish, once you've found one walleye, you've found many.

Whenever or however you take a walleye in the Canoe Country, one thing is for sure, it won't disappoint you when it comes time for a meal. Fresh walleye fillets turning a crispy brown over an open fire is one thing you won't forget when you get back home.

The Northern Pike

I don't know how many fishing trips into the wilderness have been
rescued or how often the food bag has been stretched by this fish, but I
suspect that the northern pike has accounted for more of both than can
be numbered.

It is not necessary for me to go into how much maligned the northern
pike is as a game fish. The outdoor magazines tell you about that in every
pike story they publish. The fact is that they are first on the list of
preferred fish of very few fishermen. Yet, nearly everyone has at least
one pike story they tell with much excitement. For, in truth, old *Esox
lucius* is a very exciting fish.

Catching northerns is not hard. They seem to eat just about anything and
everything. They probably got their poor reputation because small
northerns can sometimes make a nuisance of themselves when you're
fishing for some other species. Still, you never hear of anyone being
upset over catching a nice one. And most of these are accidents.
Catching big northerns consistently is a craft as difficult as any in fishing.

Pike are efficiently designed eating machines. Their elongated bodies and
rear set fins are built for rapid bursts of speed when attacking prey.
Large, sharp, pointed teeth are made for a quick grab, and their smaller,
backward slanting teeth in the roof of the mouth are there to insure that
their lunch doesn't slip away. Pike make up for any lack of beauty with
efficiency and pure savagery.

Northerns are found just about everywhere in the Canoe Country. If a
lake has nothing else in it you can bet there are at least a few northerns.
And there always seems to be one big one. Northerns have a
circumpolar distribution, a range in which the BWCAW and Quetico fall.
Though they are not one of this continent's favorite game fish they have
long been extremely popular in northern countries worldwide. The fact
that they grow even larger in Europe than here may have something to
do with it.

The largest northern taken from Minnesota waters is a monster of 45 pounds, 12 ounces, which just happened to be caught in the Canoe Country – famed Basswood Lake in 1929. In some good northern lakes the average fish may run near five pounds although the size most of us catch may be more like a couple of pounds.

Northerns live about ten years with a rare fish going on to be twenty years old. Fish older than ten years are the truly large fish. Most northerns mature sexually at three years and the bulk of spawning northerns are less than five years old.

Pike are spring spawners, usually as soon after ice-out as is possible. This occurs in April or May in the Canoe Country, all depending upon the severity of the winter and the warmth of that particular spring. Pike prefer to spawn in shallow, grassy areas, often barely deep enough to cover the adult fish. Although their spawning runs are at night they reserve the actual spawning for daylight hours. The best days for this activity have lots of sun and little wind.

When the pike have finished spawning the fishing is very good. After they move back to their summer haunts they begin to feed heavily. At that time of year the pike are most often found near early weed beds, which generally means they will be in five to eight feet of water over hard soil bottoms. They will cruise the edges of these early weed beds searching for bait fish upon which to prey. If these weeds are near channels between parts of a lake or near shallow drop-offs, so much the better. As during any time of the year, pike like to hang around stumps or fallen trees that are near or within the weed beds. If the weeds haven't sprouted yet, or the lake has few weeds as is the case in many Canoe Country lakes, the northerns will still be found near the channels, drop-offs and stumps, wherever there is sufficient cover to hide the minnows they feed on.

The nice thing about pike is that most of them are caught in less than fifteen feet of water, no matter what time of year. They also respond very well to artificial lures, a happy combination for the wandering canoeist. They like cool water, not cold, and in the Boundary Waters and

Quetico they usually don't have much of a problem finding the right temperature without having to go deep. To be sure, some large pike have been taken at great depths, but this is the exception rather than the rule.

Northerns like water less than sixty-five degrees. If the water gets over that temperature they will move toward deeper water and suspend -- which makes finding them very difficult. But even once they are suspended, pike will usually not stray too far from their early season haunts, often just sliding out into slightly deeper water in search of the right temperature. They commonly move in and out of shallow water with the rising and setting of the sun. Big northerns will come right up to shore after dark to feed even if the water temperature is considered above their ideal range. Cloudy days with a chop on the water will help keep the shallows a bit cooler and keep the pike shallow as well. When the water temperature gets over sixty-five degrees, and the pike have no access to deeper or cooler water, they will restrict their activity. Only in very shallow lakes will this be a problem.

When looking for pike on spring or early summer trips, try shallow bays with flat bottoms. These areas warm up sooner, and have early weed cover. It is not unusual to take pike in two to five feet of water in these spots at this time of year. By drifting or maneuvering slowly and quietly, and casting along weedlines or submerged logs, one should be able to raise fish. It is important to set the hook hard when you do get a strike as northerns have very bony mouths. As in all fishing, it pays to keep your hooks honed to a razor sharpness.

Use medium to shallow running plugs, spinner baits and spoons when fishing this shallow water. Try to plan your retrieve so that the lure follows the bottom contours rather than running to or away from them. Most of the time it is best to retrieve the lure briskly -- fast enough to keep it in sight just under the water's surface. Because you are fishing in shallow water it pays to keep noise in the canoe to a minimum and the presentation of the bait as quiet as possible. Heavier lures, which can be cast further from the canoe, can help hide your presence from pike.

When the northerns are in the shallows, but before water temperatures exceed sixty-five degrees, surface plugs similar to those used for largemouth bass often work well. The sight of a northern rising to smash a top water lure is one not easily forgotten. These lures are fished much the same way as just described for plugs, spinners and spoons.

Drift silently or anchor and cast the surface plug towards shore or weeds. Big pike particularly seem to like reeds. Get it as close to the land or reeds as you can. After letting the plug settle down for a minute or so, begin the retrieve. Fish the lure slowly right in the surface film and keep this up until it is right up to the rod. Often a pike will follow the lure for many yards, sizing things up. If the plug is lifted too soon from the water, or you speed up the retrieve because you think it has passed the best cover, the pike may be spooked. Give the fish time. Also, remember there is no such thing as a bad cast. Even if the lure does not land where you had intended, retrieve it with patience. We do not always know where the fish will be nor what is under the water's surface. Fish every cast as though you know there will be a strike.

There are also no hard and fast rules to fishing, and good anglers learn to experiment until they find success. If the spot looks good, and a slow retrieve has produced no strikes, try the same area using a fast retrieve. Pike sometimes strike out of pure orneriness or defensiveness and a quick retrieve can occasionally grab their attention.

Trolling for northerns can be successful. Troll near weed beds, drop-offs and submerged bars. Go slowly enough that your spoon just wobbles but doesn't spin. If you're using a plug, check its action by trolling it along the side of the canoe where you can see it. Once you've determined the trolling speed at which the lure behaves well, try to maintain that speed while fishing. When pike are shallow, you should troll with your lure about fifty or sixty feet behind the canoe. Start trolling close to the structure or weed and work your way slightly deeper if need be. You may have to add a small sinker if the fish are down ten or fifteen feet. A keel sinker will help avoid line twist. When you fish deeper it will be necessary to let out a little more line to keep the lure down.

Pike can be taken on a myriad of baits and lures, as is evidenced by the accidental catches while fishing for walleye or other fish. They will take anything from the smallest of baits and lures to large plugs, spoons or minnows. Jigs can be very effective on northerns as well. When you're fishing specifically for pike the use of a steel leader, six to ten inches in length, is a must. Their sharp teeth will saw through the heaviest of monofilament line in seconds. Try to avoid the use of these steel leaders, however, when fishing for anything else. They are highly visible to fish and the loss of a few lures to marauding northerns is not worth the diminished catches you will have if they are used while concentrating on any other fish species.

Spoons such as the Daredevle are deadly on northerns. Spoons for pike should be fairly large, between three and five inches in length. Red and white with a silver or copper belly are standard, although silver, hammered brass, blue or black and white have accounted for their share of pike as well. Light colored lures on bright days, dark on dark days, seems to be the rule. Nearly as effective as spoons are large spinners of the Mepps or Vibrax types. The addition of a buck or squirrel tail to these spinners is a real advantage as they give the lure a touch of color and life. Stick with silver or gold blades and you can't go wrong.

Pike feed mostly on small fish and minnows. Both spoons and spinners mimic these and the reason why they are such effective lures for pike. At times, minnow-like plugs (stickbaits) such as the Rapala are equally effective. These are especially productive as trolling lures although heavier sinking models can be cast into cover. Plugs for pike are best in silver, gold or perch finishes.

If you are a fly angler, and have a hankering to tie into a pike, I'd say go for it. Northerns on a fly rod are a ball. You do need a very stout rod -- I'd say at least an eight weight. Since almost all of your fly fishing will be subsurface, an intermediate density sinking line is the ticket.

The most important link in this gear is your leader. Six to eight feet of twenty to thirty pound monofilament line should be "loop-to-looped" to your fly line, with another loop at the terminal end. To that you should attach a steel leader approximately two feet long. You could also attach the steel leader to the monofilament using an Albright knot.

Flies need to be large, and sometimes flashy. Huge streamers are the norm. Attach the streamer to the steel leader by passing the leader through the eye of the hook, bending it back, and crimping it using leader crimps and a crimping pliers.

One of the best times of the year to catch really big pike is in the fall. At this time of year they are feeding heavily before the coming of winter. They move into shallower water and concentrate on schooling minnows. Fish that are normally fussy or cautious lose a considerable amount of their discretion while on these feeding binges. You would fish for these fall pike much as you would in the spring sine the pike are generally in the same shallow water areas they were at the beginning of the season. Look for good cover -- especially weed beds and reeds -- where forage fish hide. That's where the pike will be. At times in the fall, big pike will move onto stormy shores, perhaps to take advantage of the water's turbidity to aid in ambushing their prey. Don't pass up these windy shorelines even though the waves may make handling a canoe difficult, unless, of course, the conditions are unsafe. This is a case where one person should be handling the canoe while the other fishes.

Pike at all times of the year are solitary fish. Unlike other species that are schooling fish and catching one means more, catching more than one pike in a single location is rare unless bait fish are highly concentrated there. That doesn't mean that there may not be more than one pike within casting range. If the habitat is suitable for pike there may well be more than one fish around. They just won't be cozied up to each other like walleyes.

For instance, you will seldom take more than one pike from under the same log or patch of lily pads they way you might catch several bass from the same kind of cover. Make sure you cover the area thoroughly before moving on. A big, old pike may be there, just lazily watching your lure go by waiting for something that interests him. Factors such as lure color, size, depth and speed are all in your control. Experiment and be patient, he will probably strike when you've done the right things. In the long run, experimenting with different lures, speeds, etc., will get you more fish more quickly than paddling from one likely looking "hotspot" to the next, wasting valuable fishing time.

Really serious northern pike anglers often adopt tactics similar to muskie anglers – using massive stick baits or spinners to attract truly large northerns. If you're this kind of angler, you've already found that the advice above is pretty basic. Most anglers visiting the Canoe Country tend to fish for pike as a secondary species, or catch them largely by accident.

That said, if you are a serious pike chaser, you can hardly go wrong in bringing specialized pike gear to the Canoe Country. There are some truly huge northerns inhabiting these lakes, most of which have never seen a fishing lure. My recommendation would be to focus on any of the large border lakes (Crooked, Basswood, etc.) or venture into the heart of the Quetico and scour its big interior lakes. Sturgeon and Kawnipi lakes should be high up on your list. Like the border lakes, these big interior lakes are part of a flowage. All water in the Canoe Country flows north to eventually reach Hudson's Bay, but it begins by running west from north of Lake Superior. At big Saganaga Lake, the flowage splits – some

runs southwest down the international boundary through Knife Lake, Basswood, Crooked, Iron and on to Lac La Croix, while the other half flows northwest through Saganagons Lake to Kawnipi and Sturgeon before heading southwest to Lac La Croix.

These flowage lakes are particularly fertile, and I have caught many big pike in them, some large enough to require beaching the canoe while the battle took place, and more than a few that were big enough as to be scary while trying to release them. There is no doubt in my mind that a really accomplished pike angler could have a remarkable visit to any of these big flowage lakes.

For most of us, northern pike fishing is downright unscientific. Perhaps that is part of its charm. It will be a rare trip into the Canoe Country that you can't provide a few northerns for a meal if you want to. If all else fails, and you have a fish dinner on your mind, go catch a pike. Contrary to what some people say about eating northern, I have found them to be excellent from the cold, clean lakes of the north country. When of a decent size, even getting around the oft-cursed Y bones is not that hard when filleting. Instructions follow in a later chapter. With a little practice, I think you'll find that the fine eating provided by a northern pike is well worth the effort in learning how to fillet one.

Be forewarned! Catch a couple of these big, toothy critters on a canoe trip and you'll have the theme song from the old movie "Jaws" running though your mind every time you take a swim.

Canoe Country Lake Trout

In the north, in the spring, there lives a little stream.

Come summer, it barely flows; and great, gray granite boulders periscope from what little water remains, making passage by canoe nearly impossible.

But in May, this stream flows buoyantly from lake to lake, fed by melting snow. And with it flows our canoe.

Parts of the Boundary Waters are a bit too well-traveled for our tastes, but this route is seldom used. The portages, barely evident, are punctuated by moose tracks, not boot prints; and the lakes connected by this stream are rarely visited. It would not be far from the truth to say that by taking this route, we are seeing country that few human eyes have ever scanned. And we like it that way.

For decades my wife, Mary Jo, and I have chosen this route west of the Gunflint Trail for our first canoe trip of the year. Though it is not an easy route-and is growing more difficult as our bodies age-it holds a charm that offsets the effort.

The creek is part of that charm, for when traveling its hidden course, we feel a deep sense of adventure, of exploration. On the ridges along the creek, dark stands of jack pine climb the hills; and on ridges elsewhere, aspen and birch reach toward the sun.

I recall years when we waded through snow on portages and paddled through windswept channels on lakes black with rotting ice. Other years, spring came early, and the leaves -- and black flies -- had already burst forth by the time we launched our canoe.

But in most years, we find the ice has recently departed, and we must hunt north slopes to find snow -- our natural cooler for perishable foods and fresh fish fillets. Cold nights linger, keeping insects at bay. If we are lucky, the days are bright. Aspen and then birch are beginning to bud; and, thanks to those buds, the surrounding hills are awash with a soft gray-green glow, as if rubbed over with artist chalk.

It is as if the land, bound tightly for months, now sighs and breathes under the spring sun, wriggling awake like some beast arising from hibernation. Along the creek a few marsh marigolds eat light until they are as yellow as the orb that feeds them. Tiny curls of ferns shake off surrounding soil.

Everywhere is the smell of earth -- of soil, of water -- scents contained for months in winter's icy bottle. The granite bedrock of this land absorbs the sun's warmth into its billion-year-old layers.

Bears emerge from their dens, hunger dressed in black fur. Spawning suckers and pike splash in the creek. Male ruffed grouse fill the air with their drumming. Cow moose move to the safety of islands or lakeshore points to drop their tawny calves.

And, very important, lake trout move toward the water's surface, putting them in easy reach of an angler's offerings. When the aspen buds are the size of mouse ears, lake trout fishing is at its best.

If all of the other wonderful things happening in the canoe country spring weren't enough to make us paddle and portage our way to these lakes, the lure of lake trout would make sore backs and wet feet worth enduring.

Not a trout at all, *Salvelinus namaycush* is in fact a char, closely related to other northern fish species such as brook trout and arctic char. Though it lacks the red spots and brilliant coloration of these relatives, it is handsome nonetheless. The silvery fish typically has generous vermiculations along its back and irregular light spots along its sides. Some exhibit a beautiful rose-orange tint to their pectoral, pelvic, and anal fins, which may have front edges of white. The tail of the lake trout is profoundly forked.

Like Minnesotans, the lake trout is a creature of the north. It dwells only where winters are long and harsh enough to keep lakes cold despite summer's attempts to warm them. Native only to North America, the lake trout has a vast range that spans glaciated waters from Alaska east to Nova Scotia. In western Canada its range dips south through Alberta and into Montana before swinging north above the prairie and across through all eastern Canadian mainland provinces. Minnesota is about as far south as it gets.

Though moose and lynx speak to us of the north country, as do black spruce and balsam fir, the lake trout too is an indicator of climate and latitude. Like the woodland caribou, now gone but once the dominant deer in the Canoe Country, the lake trout speaks to me of wildness, of northness.

Ten thousand years ago, as the glaciers receded, leaving a rubble-strewn granite landscape, the waters that backed up behind them served as conduits for fish migrations. Were lake trout deposited in what is now southern Minnesota? No one knows. If they were, they perished as that region warmed. But where we travel each spring, the lakes, separated by stone ridges, are the guardians of lake trout evolution. Most of these lakes have never been stocked, so no gene mixing has occurred. Most lack connections, so the fish within them are direct descendants of those surviving glacial times. And the results are clear to see.

I recall one fine spring day many years ago, when Mary Jo and I portaged from our campsite lake to a neighboring body of water. We had caught a couple of lake trout for dinner from the first lake, and left them stringered off camp. These trout were dark, almost black, and nearly five pounds -- large for these small, infertile waters. In the second lake, we caught small, silvery lake trout with bright orange fins. We kept one, more out of curiosity than hunger, to compare with the others at camp; and when we placed them side by side, it was almost as if we were looking at two different species. The silvery fish was long and bullet-headed, and its flesh was as orange as any salmon's. The dark trout were much stouter, their heads blunt and round, their fillets peach in color.

Diet can explain coloration and shape to some degree, but what we were also seeing was nearly ten thousand years of natural selection, ten thousand years of time and circumstance shaping these fish to fit these lakes. A rock ridge separated them in space. But eons separated them in shape and coloration. Examining those fish, I first realized that, thanks to wilderness designations of the Boundary Waters and Quetico, here nature could choose its course without tampering.

Lake trout are one of the main reasons the BWCAW and Quetico are so popular with anglers. After all, you can catch walleyes, northerns and smallmouth bass elsewhere. But with the exceptions of the Great Lakes, the Northeast and a few scattered areas where they have been introduced, this region contains the most southerly concentration of good lake trout lakes.

Lakers are also a fish made for daydreaming. They can and do grow to huge size and while these big fish are not the ones that make up the bulk of our catch there is always the chance and hope that we will tie into one. Lake trout well over twenty pounds lurk in the depths of some Canoe Country lakes. It doesn't take too much imagination to picture one of these grey monsters being subdued along side of your canoe.

Many people labor under the common misconception that you can only catch lake trout on light tackle in the spring. Their belief is that during the summer one must use heavy tackle and trolling to take lake trout, both of which are synonymous with work when fishing from a canoe with no motor. This is not strictly true. While spring is the easiest time to catch lakers, you can take them throughout the summer on light tackle with methods we'll get to later in this chapter.

Some of my fondest fishing memories of the Boundary Waters center on spring lake trout trips. Our family traditionally made these early season trips as far back as I can remember, starting with my father who explored these waters back in the late 1940s. One trip in particular sticks out in my mind. It had been a late spring, the kind that make for good lake trout fishing since the surface water remains cold until the season opener. Snow could easily be found on shadowy hillsides and was a great natural refrigerator of lake trout fillets. Poplar trees cast the first faint

tinges of new green on the landscape, their small leaves a bright contrast to the deep greens of the pines and spruce. The nights were still chilly enough to freeze the water bottles and make a popsicle of last evening's left over coffee, the kind of nights that, if it wasn't for the thought of those lake trout awaiting, you might never have gotten out of your sleeping bag.

The lake, to remain nameless, couldn't have lost its ice more than a few days before we had arrived. The water was a uniform cold throughout and the lake trout were taking advantage of the warming rays of the sun by feeding heavily along shallow shores and over reefs. A hundred yards or so from the campsite was a reef, marked by what we always referred to as the "sea gull" rock. True to its name there were always sea gulls resting and nesting on the bare protrusion.

This reef is typical of those found in Canoe Country lakes. It begins at the rock, dropping down into about ten feet of water rather quickly and gradually gets deeper before reaching our island campsite. Along its length you can take lake trout most of the season because it offers the right depth somewhere except, perhaps, during the hottest stretches of the summer.

By taking advantage of the wind and quietly drifting parallel to the reef, casting spoons or bouncing a jig, we took a laker on nearly every cast for the three days we fished. Occasionally, a marauding northern was hooked or sheared off our lures. The fishing was so good that it didn't seem to make much difference what color lure you tossed at them but the fish did show a decided preference to a lure tipped with a small minnow, an occurrence I've found repeated many times with lake trout.

This is spring lake trout fishing at its best. It is one of the fastest types of fishing there is providing you get the right set of conditions. It is important to fish as soon as possible after ice out, fishing season permitting. At this time of year the water is cold enough for the lake trout to be in what is normally shallow water for them, giving anglers a chance to fish them easily on light tackle. The fish move up onto the reefs and shores to take advantage of the better feed and perhaps to find a little warmer water. During a normal spring the warmest water at this time is not too warm for lake trout.

The key water temperature to look for in the spring is about forty degrees Fahrenheit. A small pocket thermometer can be helpful in locating water at or about this temperature. Failing to bring a thermometer, try fishing in three to ten feet of water and work deeper if no fish are found. Of course, this advice is of no use if the spring has been early or quickly warms up. I remember one trip where the air temperature shot up to eighty degrees during the first week of fishing season and stayed there the whole time we were out. It quickly drove the fish down and we were lucky to have had along some heavier sinkers in order to reach the fish. Remember that and always throw in some extra heavy sinkers.

The average spring, however, will find the lake trout in shallow water until the first week of June. The earlier you get there the shallower they will be. You should be able to find them on their favorite haunts which, generally speaking, have two points in common: lake trout like rocks and rubble, and rarely are they found in weedy areas or over bare, smooth bottoms.

Lake trout also prefer to have access to deep water and will not be found too far from it. A reef that drops off into the depths will usually have more fish on it than a reef of the same depth that bottoms out quickly. Large lake trout seem to be found nearer the deep water than will the smaller fish. Look for islands or points that may have rocky reefs extending out into the lake. Shorelines with similar structure running parallel to it are also good locations to try. At this time of year the lakers will seldom be deeper than fifteen feet, providing the weather hasn't been too warm. Right after ice-out they can be very nearly right up amongst the rocks on shore in only two feet of water! Since they are so light and temperature conscious, try cruising the shallows at dawn and dusk because that will be exactly what the lakers should be doing.

Unless you are adept at recognizing good lake trout waters, a great aid would be a topographic map of your chosen lake or a small fish locator. These will help you locate the reefs and shorelines on which you should be concentrating your efforts. If a map or locator is unavailable, don't despair. Fishermen caught fish for centuries without maps and electronic gear by using their brains and powers of observation. Study the shoreline. A steep cliff along the bank probably means the same is under water, a situation not conducive to good lake trout fishing unless (and rarely) falling rocks have piled up to form a reef. Low, flat areas running down to the shore suggest a bar or reef of similar nature beneath the surface. If the shore of this is composed of rock and rubble, chances are you've found a good place to start. Those sloping rock shelves so common to these Canadian Shield lakes, the ones as smooth as an elephant's back, seldom belie good fish cover below, no matter what the species you're after. If the trout lake you are on has a stream entering it, especially if it and where it dumps in are rocky, you may have found another hotspot.

Water color can tell about what is underneath. Deep water in these lakes tends to be very dark while water over reefs is light, often with a blue-green cast. In short, in the spring you are looking for rocky areas in water anywhere from five to fifteen feet deep. The best spots will have access to deeper water along one or both sides.

Once you have found this type of spot you can work it in a couple of different ways. Probably the best way to ascertain where the fish are is by trolling along or over the spot. This allows you to cover a lot of water relatively quickly until you locate the fish. Once found, you can continue to troll over the fish but your best bet is to anchor, as repeated passes over fish in these clear lakes may spook them.

When trolling let out plenty of line; a hundred feet being a minimum. This helps because any fish spooked by your passing will have time to settle down before your lure comes by. Speed is important. Generally speaking, one must troll slowly for lake trout, not perhaps as slow as for walleyes, but still slow. Most people troll too fast. If both you and your partner are paddling very easily, your speed should be about right. Another factor is the type of spoon or plug you are trolling with. Each lure has a speed at which it works best and all in the canoe should have on compatible lures. Try watching your lure alongside the canoe for a few minutes. A spoon should flutter from side to side but never spin. A plug should wobble like the minnow it mimics. Once you have determined the proper speed, let out your line and try to maintain that pace. When fishing deep, or with a lot of line, it is OK to pick up the pace slightly.

After locating a good spot, or perhaps after picking up your first lake trout, work the area over methodically. Lakers are not as much of a schooling fish as walleyes, but when one is encountered chances are you will find more in close proximity. If your initial technique does not prove successful again, experiment by moving slightly shallower or deeper or by varying lure speed. Prove to yourself that there are no more fish there before moving on. In the long run it will produce more fish than will running all over the lake.

If you have found a "honey hole", your choices of how to fish it are relatively few. Anchoring just off to the side and casting to them with spoons, jigs, plugs or flies is the most productive. This technique spooks the fish the least while keeping you on top of the hole. It is better to work the structure by fishing parallel to it rather than toward or away from it. When fishing parallel to a reef you can best control your lure depth, which sometimes is critical. Casting to or away from structure often leaves your lure angling away from the proper depth. Few strikes will be had if the lure is passing above the fish's head.

Wind, which is often the canoeist's bane, can also be made to work in your favor when fishing. Suppose you have found a suitable point or reef and have figured out what depth the lakers are at. If there is a breeze blowing in a direction that is parallel or even quartering the structure, you can use it to carry you silently over the fish. In this manner you can either slowly bounce a jig along the bottom, or you can take casts with spoons and spinners. This allows you to cover more water with a minimum of effort, which is a desirable combination unless you really like to paddle all day.

If the fish are ten or fifteen feet deep, you should have no worries about spooking them while drifting over. However, if they are shallower than this, try to plan your drift to come alongside where you believe the fish to be, and cast to them. Canoe Country lakes can be extremely clear and the shadow of your canoe passing over may send the fish scurrying to the depths. A slight chop on the water, which is usually the case when drift fishing, will help cut down on this effect.

As mentioned before, be creative. Although lake trout are not the most demanding of fish, you may have to vary your lure speed, color or depth in order to entice repeated strikes. It is far less a waste of time to do this than it is trying to fish the entire lake at one time, especially when you have no motor. Crossing even a two hundred acre lakes while use up much of your valuable fishing time.

The most consistent lures for spring and early summer fishing are spoons, Mepps-type spinners and jigs. Lake trout feed mostly on minnows and bait fish such as suckers and whitefish, and these lures best imitate them. Spoons are easy to cast in the 1/2 to 7/8 ounce sizes. The best colors are the old standbys of silver, gold, brass, copper or any combination of these. A dash of fluorescent orange on the spoons can be very effective at times. Jigs are best in white, yellow, chartreuse and black in sizes 1/2 and 1 ounce. Spinners should be in any of the same colors as the spoons, and their bucktails should be of the same colors as the jigs. A size three Mepps, give or take a size, is nearly perfect. If you are fishing in the Boundary Waters, where bait is still legal, I've found that adding a small minnow hooked through the head to any lure increases the number of strikes. If you don't have bait, or are in the

Quetico, you might want to give your lure a shot of one of the commercial fish attractant scents available. Although I've never seen a study proving it one way or another, my experience tells me that lake trout use their noses more than any other fish in the north country.

Minnow imitating plugs such as the Rapala, in bright finishes and colors, are very effective for taking lake trout. My absolute favorite is the original floating Rapala, model F07 or F09, in orange and gold. Lake trout just can't seem to refuse it. When trolling with plugs, a sinker of the proper size is often needed to get the lure down and should be placed two or three feet up the line. Bead chain sinkers, such as the keel type, will help to avoid line twist. In addition to plugs, spoons designed for trolling should be in your box. Unlike spoons designed for casting, trolling spoons are light in weight. They are sometimes called "flutter spoons" and must have some weight added three feet or more up your line to keep them down at the proper depth. Old fashioned silver or gold colors are hard to beat, but they come in a lot of colors. Take a look at a catalog, or visit a bait shop, that caters to anglers fishing the Great Lakes and you'll find a wide selection of these spoons.

Casting with spoons is also very productive, and the brand and model is less important than the size or weight. Spoons designed for casting are heavier than trolling spoons, and generally shorter. You'll want spoons that weigh at least a quarter ounce, and most should be one half ounce or three eighths of an ounce. Some of the most productive spoons over the years have been the Doctor, Daredevle in its many variations, and the Luhr Jensen Krocodile (my favorite casting spoon). Force me to choose just two colors for lakers, and I'd pick spoons that were brass or gold with some fluorescent orange on them, or silver spoons with a dash of blue.

Another technique, often overlooked, that can be very productive and exciting for taking lake trout is with the use of a flyrod and flies. When lake trout are in the shallows there is absolutely no reason a fly can't compete with the other lures. Most people think of fly fishing as dry fly or stream fishing only, including many fly fishermen. Yet with the use of a large streamer, lake trout can be fished very successfully on a fly rod. Since they are so shallow in the spring a weighted streamer on a floating line is often all that is needed, although I always throw in a sinking tip line just in case. A seven or eight weight rod and line is all that is needed and if you prefer you can even go lighter since you have plenty of room to play the fish. Seven to nine foot tapered leaders with a 3X tippet complete the tackle.

Streamers are the best choice since they imitate minnows. Hook size is not so important as is the length of the dressing on the hook. Brightly dressed flies in gold, grey, silver, red and thousands of combinations and other colors will all work. Hook size need not be large but as a minimum size I would recommend an eight. Sixes and fours would be the norm and are best in a long shank if for no other reason than the ease in tying the fly. Some like to tie in a trailing stinger hook.

Large, flashy streamers are the ticket, and just like the plugs and spoons, I like streamers that have silver, gold, orange and/or blue in them. With the many synthetic hairs and plastic fibers available to fly tyers these days, there's no reason you can't concoct some truly juicy and flashy looking flies for lakers. Zonker-type flies are great, and bright colored wooly buggers are a close second. Variations on traditional lake streamers, such as the Black Nosed Dace and Mickey Finn work well too. Just about any of these flies and others two or more inches long, snaked amongst the rocks in which lake trout forage can result in successive strikes. It is pure joy to hook a nice laker on a fly rod, and is just about the most fun you can have sitting up in a canoe. A note about fly rod length: the longer the better. Keeping your back cast off the water while sitting in a canoe can be difficult and a long rod is an aid.

In early to midsummer, before the lakes have warmed up too terribly much, lake trout can usually be found in twenty to fifty feet of water. At these depths, which are not considered extreme for lake trout, you can fish much the same way you would for spring lake trout. The major difference is how much weight you must attach in order to get the lure down to the fish.

Start by finding the same or similar reefs you would look for in the spring. Many of these will have deeper stretches along their lengths. During this first month of the summer, lake trout may be as shallow as fifteen to twenty feet, especially at dawn and dusk. Once you have located a good looking reef or point proceed to fish as described earlier for spring lakers. Locating the fish is the one variable that makes taking lake trout a bit more difficult than in the spring, but once found they will still bite readily.

If you have no map or fish locator and are at a loss as to where to start fishing, a good method is to do a little "sounding" yourself. While drifting or paddling slowly, bounce a fair sized jig along the bottom. By bouncing along in this manner you are sounding the bottom for reefs and drop-offs. At the same time you stand a good chance of hooking a fish. While this method is slow, it is time honored and often overlooked since the invention of fish locators.

If you are bottom bouncing, pay close attention to what you are feeling on the end of your line. You want to be aware of changes in the lake's bottom and be able to construct some kind of mental image of what it looks like down there. If you detect an abrupt change in the topography, a few passes should indicate which way the reef runs. Take some bearing from landmarks and start fishing as you would in spring with adjustments in tackle for depth.

Fishing at greater depths is really no more difficult than fishing shallower waters and only requires more heavily weighted lures, more time to allow for the lure to sink, and more attention to possible strikes. Because of the depth, strikes will feel softer. Monofilament line also will stretch giving a duller sensation. Just keep your line tight and set on any hesitation. Set HARD.

As the summer progresses most people give up on lake trout fishing. The feeling is that since the fish are so deep, anywhere from 35 to 100 feet down, they are impossible to catch. Most believe you must have in your possession deep trolling equipment, that is, wire line, heavy rods and diving planes. The truth be known, even if you did haul all this specialized trolling gear with you it would be extremely difficult to handle without a motor. With all this on the end of your line it would indeed be quite a chore to paddle.

When lake trout are down at such depths, fishing *is* more difficult. But it is not so hard that, if you wish to catch lakers, it is impossible. There are ways, on your summer trips, to catch lake trout that allow you to use the same basic equipment you brought along for the rest of your fishing. While these techniques might work better on equipment specifically designed for them (short, stiff rod and braided, non-stretching line) the name of the game when you are this far back in the bush is versatility. Your equipment can handle these chores and you can take lake trout from a hundred feet of water. The method is nothing more than vertical jigging -- virtually the same technique you would use for ice fishing. The most difficult thing about it is locating the trout. The actual technique is easy.

Summer lake trout are usually below the lake's thermocline. In many lakes there is little or no oxygen below the thermocline, but in lake trout lakes these depths have plenty of oxygen. This is what makes them trout lakes. It is at these depths that the lake trout find the temperature they desire, a chilly 48 to 54 degrees Fahrenheit.

The trick is to locate the fish at these extreme depths. As mentioned before, a topographic map of the lake is a great aid as would be a fish locator. Remember that, just like in the spring, the good spots are not covering the entire bottom of the lake. It is not a hopeless task even though it may seem that way when looking at the large expanse of the lake's surface. There will be areas that will concentrate the trout due to structure and food.

The best spots will be as near as possible to the early summer reefs, bars, and points. If you recall, I wrote that the best spring reefs were the ones that had access to deep water. Lakers are found on those reefs in the spring not because they need access to the depths at that time, but because they move down the reef with the coming of hot weather and warm water. Lake trout are not very migratory in nature. They are much more likely to move up and down in a lake, than to wander across it. For that reason, reefs that run from shallow to deep are always the best choice, no matter the time of year.

Once you've found what looks like a promising place to fish, use the wind (or paddle slowly) to bounce a lure along the bottom. When doing this bottom bouncing routine go as slowly as possible. Too much slant in your line will mean infrequent contact with the bottom. Your monofilament line is going to be doing a lot of stretching at these depths, so your jigging motions must be greatly exaggerated and done with force to really lift that jig.

You can, by the way, do this technique with a spoon if you add plenty of weight. On a dropper from the bottom of a three way swivel, about a foot or more long, attach three to six ounces of weight. At one of the other rings tie in the line from your reel. Then tie on a leader to the opposite end, making it about three feet long. To this apply your chosen spoon (or plug). This rig has two advantages over attaching the sinkers directly to your line. First, it allows the lure to rise a couple feet off the bottom above the weight, making it easier for the fish to see. Secondly, if you do hang up, chances are it will be the sinker, not the lure. By using lighter line on the dropper than what is on your reel, or by attaching sinkers that can slide on the line, you will hopefully only break the dropper or slide off the sinkers thereby saving the lure.

Jigs must be jigged viciously about the length of your rod. Spoons can be pumped up and down a bit more leisurely, three to four feet at a time. When you feel a touch down, lift immediately. A strike at these depths will not feel like much, just a heaviness to the line. Often lake trout will grab a lure as it flutters down as you drop the rod tip. Pay attention, when you lift again, for a slight hesitation, a heavy feeling. That's a laker! Set the hook and set it HARD because line stretches at these depths!

Once you have found the fish, stay put. If there is no wind, you can drift, but your best bet is to anchor. You want to be able to jig right on top of the fish. Using 1/2 to 1 ounce jigs or heavy spoons. Lures designed for ice fishing work well, such as the Heddon Sonar, Swedish pimple, or Rapala Jigging Shad Rap. Lift the rod quickly to its full length and then drop it sharply, letting the lure flutter down. Any slight hesitation as you lift may be a fish. When in doubt, just set the hook, and set it hard. It helps to hone your hooks and keep them sharp as all the stretch in your line at these depths will make hooking a bit more difficult. A sharp hook can make all the difference in the world.

The lure colors for deep lake trout are the same as at any other depth with one exception. For some reason, and I don't claim to know why, black jigs work very well.

If you are visiting the Canoe Country from some region where lake trout aren't found, I'd urge you to give angling for them a serious try. These beautiful, wild fish are often highly colored and sometimes look more like their cousin the brook trout. Living in these cold, clean waters, these inland lake trout usually have red to salmon colored flesh, although some lakes contain fish with white meat. All are delicious.

The average size is around three pounds, but many lakers in the ten to twenty pound class have been taken, with a few going even larger. Every trout lake seems to have a different subspecies, with color and size varying widely.

With a little luck, some perseverance, and these guidelines you should be able to land some of these beautiful fish of the north.

Backwoods Bronzebacks

It was one of those incredibly hot and muggy summer days when the effort of any activity would send stinging sweat running down your forehead and into your eyes.

All day long the sun had played hide and seek with ominous black rain clouds, disappearing with the coming of repetitive and sudden thundershowers. When the sun would reappear, so would the mosquitoes and flies, buzzing lazily toward their victims as if they too were stifled by the heat. Through all of this, with occasional runs to shore when lightning was threatening, we continued to fish for smallmouth.

The weather wasn't what one hopes for on a canoe trip. It also wasn't weather normally conducive to good fishing. Yet after every sudden storm, as the sun came back, so did the smallmouth. Tentatively at first, like the sun, and then aggressively, smashing every bait thrust at them. Most were large fish, running two to three pounds, perhaps recovering more quickly than their little fellows to take advantage of the momentary calm to wolf down some lunch. For this day and the next we caught smallmouth after smallmouth whenever we could venture back onto the lake.

The fishing saved that trip, for despite the weather, which continued to be rotten unless you like being wet, hot and bug bitten all at the same time, we were reluctant to go home and leave the tremendous fishing we were enjoying. And while this kind of weather is not the kind to look for if you're going smallmouth bass fishing, it perhaps teaches us the lesson that nothing about catching fish is a sure bet. If we had paid attention to our natural inclination, which was to curl up in the shade and read a book, we would have missed some very good fishing.

I doubt that you could find much more exciting fishing, or faster action than, tying into a mess of smallmouth bass. This member of the black bass family, with the scientific mouthful name of *Micropterus dolomieui*, provides one of the most exciting fishing opportunities in the Canoe Country.

Although smallmouth are not large in size – typical Canoe Country smallmouth are under two pounds – these bronze beauties make up for any lack of size in sheer fighting ability.

When I was but a tad of a lad I saw my father battle the first smallmouth I had ever seen. We were fishing one of the big border lakes when he hooked this fish on a yellow hair jig (I remember that well since I insisted he tie an identical jig on my line as soon as he landed the fish) that had been tipped with a minnow. I thought he hooked a tarpon! This fish went crazy, leaping time and time again, each time shaking its head trying to throw that jig. I had only seen a fish behave like that once before, that being in an old movie depicting tarpon fishing, hence my astute identification of his fish. When my dad finally subdued that smallmouth it was obvious to even the untrained eye that this was a big fish. It went over five pounds. My father had caught plenty of fish by this time in his life, though I suspect the numbers of fish declined as the number of children's lines he had to tie, bait and untangle grew, but I still remember his excitement at landing this bass. It wasn't often I saw him get that worked up over something that wasn't my fault.

That's what so fun about smallmouth. Each one, down to those hardly bigger than your lure, is a born battler. For the most part they are also pretty easy to catch, a combination hard to resist. For those who claim they don't like to eat bass, you're in for a big surprise when you sit down to a meal of fresh smallmouth fillets. Taken from the cool waters they love so much, smallmouth are a delight to munch on.

Smallmouth bass really seem to have little in common with their largemouth cousin. Smallmouth much prefer the cool waters of these northwoods lakes and, rather than hiding in the weedy back bays like the largemouth, they are found in clear water over rocky bottoms or in cascading streams. In appearance smallmouth are distinguished from largemouth by an upper jaw that does not extend back past the eye. Fin placement and body configuration are nearly identical to the largemouth but smallmouth are usually brown to bronze in color with dark vertical

bars, although I have found some lakes in the Canoe Country where the bars are nearly absent and the fish almost a golden hue, and in others, nearly black.

Despite the fact that they are widespread, smallmouth are not native to the area. They were introduced some years ago and have been spreading their range ever since. If there is a waterway connecting two lakes it is only a matter of time and high water until they find their way from one to another. If they find their new home to their liking they will quickly establish themselves. Many former strictly lake trout lakes now have smallmouth populations, to the chagrin of some fishermen and delight of others, since both fish like the cool, clear waters and rubble bottoms. In most cases they coexist well together, the laker using the depths of the lake and the bass the shallows.

Since I first wrote this book in 1984, smallmouth have continued to expand their range. Lakes that had no smallmouth at that time now have resident populations. For instance, I've fished the Kawishiwi River system (north of Malberg Lake) for decades. Walleyes and northern pike were always present, as well as some surprisingly big bluegills. But it wasn't until about five years ago that I first hooked a smallmouth in that area. Whether or not the bass will fare well there remains to be seen – in some lakes into which they have expanded they simply exist as a small population of runts.

Smallmouth are spring spawners, which means, in the Quetico and BWCAW, June. On some cold years you will sometimes catch smallmouth into July that have yet to spawn, their round bellies still swollen with eggs. The depth at which they spawn varies and is determined by water temperature and clarity. They will spawn in water as shallow as a foot or as deep as twenty, wherever they find suitable conditions. The majority of spawning will happen in the shallower end of that range.

The smallmouth's nest is built by the male and they can be extremely territorial at this time. Spawning activities will peak when water temperature reaches the sixties, and if you cruise the shoreline you can often see, with the aid of polarized sunglasses, smallmouth on their spawning beds. These beds appear as a lighter colored dish or bowl, often up to three feet across, on the gravel bottoms.

Usually, smallmouth are found in rocky lakes with a minimum depth of twenty-five to thirty feet. They like summertime water temperatures of sixty to eighty degrees. Smallies feed mostly on insects and their larvae, as well as crayfish and minnows. Even in the warmest of weather they are almost never found below the thirty foot range and more often than not are found in less than fifteen feet of water. While they can run quite small in some lakes, the Minnesota record is eight pounds. Each year fish close to that record are taken with many four and five pounders being caught. Any smallmouth over a couple of pounds is a handful on light tackle.

Before the water gets up to seventy degrees the smallmouth will be in eight feet of water or less. They will take surface baits avidly at this time and always prefer small lures or bait. They will also feed voraciously on mayfly hatches. If you are a fly angler, never, I repeat, never leave your flyrod at home at anytime of the season if you're headed into smallmouth waters.

When making an early season venture into the Canoe Country, May through the end of June most years, you will find smallmouth in shallow waters. Even though they like cool water, small mouth will be found in the warmer parts of these cold lakes. This means the shallow shorelines, bays and reefs. Never pass up the chance to fish the mouth of a creek or stream that may be dumping into a bass lake, especially while the water is still cool. These flowing waters wash an abundance of food to the smallmouth and are popular feeding areas even though the lake surrounding the creek's entry point may not appear to be ideal bass cover. Some of the larger streams, if they have good flow and rapids, will have smallmouth in them all year round, and in this respect they are very trout-like.

When trying to decide where to fish for smallmouth, start by looking for shores and points with plenty of rocks and rubble. Not those smooth rock shelves, mind you. They are very poor cover for smallmouth or the critters they feed on. What you are looking for are areas with rocks the size of your fist to the size of your head. If this spot has occasional large boulders dropped there by the untidy receding glaciers, that's OK. Just

be sure the bulk of it is made up of the smaller rocks.

Smallmouth hunt in these rocky areas for crayfish, a favorite food, and it provides cover for minnows and insect larvae. All in all, these rubble reefs, shores and points offer the smallmouth a veritable smorgasbord of entrees. You really wouldn't expect them to be anywhere else, would you?

A nice thing about most smallmouth lakes is that because of the water clarity you can often find the right structure just by peering down into the water on the shadowy side of the canoe. Polarized sunglasses are a tremendous aid, allowing you to clearly see the bottom by cutting the glare. At times you will actually see the fish finning lazily along or streaking away.

Smallmouth structure is a lot like that for walleyes in the northwoods lakes. They like drop-offs and at times will suspend off them as would a walleye. They most often congregate on reefs and the like that have a range of depths, so that they can move up or down them according to the water temperature or sunlight. For most of the season you will find them if you seek them in ten to fifteen feet of water. It is pretty common to find both walleye and smallmouth on the same reef – usually the smallmouth will be found in slightly shallower water.

In the early months shallow bays can often be hotspots. Because they warm more quickly and usually have lush insect and minnow life, they are attractive to smallmouth while the water is still reasonably cool. It pays to check out bays that appear too muddy or weedy for smallmouth, especially if you're having a tough time on the typical structures. Some of these bays may contain a small area of suitable smallmouth habitat and, because of the food and temperature, be a temporary home to them while the water remains cool, often concentrating the bass. Watch for small stretches of rock shoreline or rock piles.

When the bass are in the shallows, perhaps the most exciting way to fish for them is with surface lures and flies. Smallmouth readily take small surface plugs. Even later in the summer they will move back into the shallows at dawn and dusk to take advantage of an insect hatch, again making surface baits ideal.

If you are a spin fisherman, small plugs such as the floating Rapala, or my very favorite, the old standby Heddon Tiny Torpedo, work very well. Just remember to keep the lure size to about half the size you think it should be. Smallmouth love small baits. A lure about 1-3/4 to 2 inches in length is about right.

Most surface fishing is done along shorelines and the best types for this have a combination of rubble, gradually tapering depth and fallen trees in the water. Once found, approach the area as quietly as possible. If there are two of you fishing, it is really much better if you take turns, one person paddling to maintain position. The bow person should swing around to face the stern paddler, in effect making both ends of the canoe a stern end. By doing so, each fisherman has complete control over the canoe when it becomes his time to set down the rod and man the paddle. In this respect the canoe is one of the most versatile of all fishing crafts, quick and easy to maneuver. With just one person at a time fishing, the paddler can quickly back the canoe out of the cover while the fishing

SMALLMOUTH TIPS

-- *SMALLMOUTH LIKE HARD, ROCK STREWN BOTTOMS.*

-- *SHORELINES WITH FALLEN TREES ARE GREAT SPOTS.*

-- *SMALL, RATHER THAN BIG, LURES ARE BEST.*

-- *JUNE IS THE BEST MONTH FOR SURFACE FISHING.*

-- *EVEN IN AUGUST, SMALLMOUTH WILL RARELY BE DEEPER THAN FIFTEEN FEET.*

partner fights the fish free of obstructions. If you need to scoot in a few yards to make that cast, no sweat. A couple of light paddle strokes from your partner and you're there, with no noise or commotion to spook fish. On calm days with clear water, the quiet of a canoe and its low profile are both big advantages over motorboats. It can make all the difference in your fishing success.

Make your cast as close to shore as is feasible without hanging it in a tree. Let the lure sit quietly on the surface for a minute or so. I really mean a minute, not just a few seconds. Some fish are frightened by the splash down of the plug, others merely intrigued by it. In either case, a wait of a minute will allow them to recover and has been proven, at least to my satisfaction, to increase strikes.

A slow retrieve is in order. As soon as the lure touches the water's surface, pick up the slack and then wait. You want to be ready to set the hook and slack in the line will make this very difficult. Keep your rod tip low, and pointed at the lure.

Most surface plugs are designed to create a disturbance and gurgling noise. Too fast a retrieve will destroy the intended action of the plug and may turn fish away. You want the plug to sputter and inch along, hoping it appears to the bass as a desirable, but crippled, critter. Plugs like the Rapala, not really intended to be surface plugs, work admirably at this task if you know how to handle them. Cast the Rapala toward shore, as you would any plug, and let it sit. When you begin your retrieve, give it a short jerk to one side, and then reel up the slack. The plug will dive a couple of inches and then surface again, the diving lip at its head giving off a sputtering sound as it pulls air down with it. Repeat this sequence, with a short jerk now to the opposite side, all the way back to the canoe. This technique is called "walking the dog." Using this method, a floating stick bait displays the struggle of a wounded minnow, and will seldom be passed up once spotted by a bronzeback. When doing any surface fishing, keep the slack out of your line at all times. The sudden swirl of a rising bass can be a shock and you must set hard and instantly. Slack will be your number one nemesis.

When there is an insect hatch on, the surface of the lake can be boiling with rising smallmouth. At these times you can see the rings of the feeding fish or hear the splash of an overly exuberant one. After chasing from one rise to the next, it is my experience that the smallest fish make the most noise. The big ones are content to just sip in the bugs.

If you enjoy fly fishing, this is an opportunity hard to pass up. Smallmouth bass are exciting game on a flyrod, and even when there isn't a hatch going on, they respond favorably to flies most of the season. If I told you about evenings where just about any fly on every cast resulted in a least a strike, if not a fish on, you may not believe me. But it has happened, and often enough to prove it is not just a chance occurrence. It is at times like this that an angler with a flyrod can easily out fish his spinning counterpart, although both will probably catch all the fish they want.

When fly fishing for smallmouth on the surface just about any surface bug, whether of deer hair or cork, will take fish. Stick to the smaller sizes of traditional bass bugs with sizes six and eight being about right. I have not found smallmouth to be terribly color conscious, but I have noted that they prefer light, natural colors to bright reds, whites or yellows. It will also payoff to throw in some traditional dry flies in order to match any mayfly hatch you might encounter. These hatches are sporadically spread through the middle of June into early July. Because the weather this far north can never be counted on, a cold year, or even a cold few weeks, can result in the hatches being delayed until much later than usual. Since flies weigh almost nothing and take little space, it is worth it to throw a few in even if you suspect there may be no hatches at the time of your canoe trip. They will also serve double duty if you decide to

stop at one of the stream trout lakes scattered around the Boundary Waters. More on these lakes later.

It is also interesting to note that lakes on the far eastern edge of the wilderness, nearer Lake Superior, tend to stay cooler longer, and have later insect hatches than lakes further west. My best guess is that there may be as much as a two week difference between lakes in the vicinity of Lac la Croix and those located off the Arrowhead Trail. I've seen astounding hatches of *Hexagenia Limbata* (a huge mayfly) on lakes off the Arrowhead Trail as late as mid-July in some cool years. Typically these mayflies hatch in mid-June.

For fly fishing under the surface throw in some streamer flies – Zonkers and Wooly Buggers being the best bets. Since smallmouth are in relatively shallow water so much of the time, you are not at much of a disadvantage using fly equipment. In fact at times it will be an advantage, because flies can often better imitate what bass are feeding on than hard plastic plugs. A floating weight forward or bug taper and a sinking tip weight forward will be all you need. Since size and weight of gear is everything on a canoe trip, I've more recently taken to leaving the sink-tip line at home and now just carry a sinking line "mini-head" which just attaches via loop-to-loop to the tip of the floating fly line.

Leaders do not have to be too long – seven and a half footers work just fine – and should taper to about a 3X tippet. A few of those ultra tiny split shot tossed in your kit will be handy to help keep those streamer flies near the bottom if the need should arise. Keeping your back cast off the water is tougher in a canoe than when wade fishing or standing in a boat, so a long rod (nine foot) is nice. I like a seven weight rod for this kind of fly fishing, but a six or eight weight would work just fine.

Whether you use flies or lures, make your retrieve all the way back to the canoe. Bass will come up out of ten feet of water to take a top water or shallow running lure, so don't pull it out of the water just because it passed the shallow area without a strike. It is not uncommon to see two or three fish following your lure and many times a smallmouth will follow it quite a distance before deciding to strike. It is a peculiarity of smallmouth to even follow the fish you've hooked, running and dodging with it, right up to the canoe.

The spin fisherman will do well with the basic tackle we discussed earlier: a medium weight rod and reel. If you are going in strictly after smallmouth, a light or ultra-light rod and reel can do the job and will be a ball to use. Your reel should be filled to the brim with line. By doing so you will be able to cast a greater distance with ease, an ability that may be important when the fish are right up on the shoreline on a dead calm evening, and when approaching too near may spook the bass. Six pound test line is more than adequate for smallmouth, or just about anything else, and will cast further and easier than eight or ten pound line.

When the smallmouth are not on the surface or in the shallows along shore, begin your search in slightly deeper water, gradually working your way ten or fifteen feet deep. Stormy weather can put smallmouth down deep, but they will come back up once the weather settles. No matter what the case, stick to the rules and look for those rocky reefs and points. In deep water as well as shallow, smallmouth will be on these types of structures.

Some of the best lures to use when fishing these deeper areas for smallmouth are small spinners. The Mepps and Vibrax spinners are deadly on smallmouth and are especially effective because the spinning blades seem to keep the lure from hanging up in those rock gardens. Spinners in size one and two are the best. Black, silver or gold blades will do. I like the ones with the squirrel tails and believe that they are more effective. Besides, they're prettier. Crawl these lures through the rocks with an occasional touchdown and you'll take bass.

I've found that an effective method of fishing a squirrel tail Mepps for smallmouth is to throw them parallel to shore and let them sink to the bottom. A slow, pumping retrieve makes the hair tail flare out, a motion I believe causes the bass to mistake the lure for their favorite food, crayfish. Since the blade revolves in front of the hooks, it acts as a guard, lifting the spinner over obstructions so that, even though you are fishing right on the bottom, snags are not as frequent as you might think. This technique works especially well after the smallmouth have moved into deeper water and by casting parallel to shore, as opposed to casting to shore (shallow water) and retrieving to the canoe (deep water), the spinner will spend more time at the same depth as the fish.

When smallmouth are no longer actively taking surface lures, but are still shore oriented, casting to shore from a canoe with a diving plug similar to the Rapala Shad Rap is hard to beat. Since these types of fast diving

plugs dive deeper the faster they are retrieved, reeling faster as the retrieve progresses toward you keeps the lure diving. It helps to hold your rod tip low as well. The key here is to put, and keep, the lure where the fish are. Perch and crawdad finishes have turned out to be exceptional smallmouth plugs.

Another favorite smallmouth bass lure is the jig. Most of these lures are available with or without a spinner blade attached above the jig proper. While they are effective without the blade, I believe the flashing blade attracts fish from a greater distance and therefore accounts for more strikes. Any jig for smallmouth bass should be about an eighth to a quarter ounce in weight. The best colors are brown, black, purple, yellow and orange. Replacement bodies for these jigs are available and it is a good idea to throw some in your tackle box. A marauding northern can tear these soft plastic bodies to pieces and even smallmouth are not always easy on them. With a bunch of extra bodies along you'll be able to repair them without having to tie on a whole new lure. You will also be able to change color without going through the whole routine of cutting one off and tying on another.

I no longer use live bait for smallmouth (and you can't take or use organic bait in the Quetico anyway) but there's no question that leeches and nightcrawlers are deadly on bass.

The best method is to use a small bait hook with these baits (about a size six short shank) fished below a slip bobber. A small split shot sinker will be needed to keep the bait at the right depth. You can also use a "Lindy" type rig with slip sinkers. In either case, keep in mind that smallmouth tend to really inhale live bait. You're going to find that you've hooked some of these fish pretty deep in the gullet. Don't force the hook out if you're planning to release fish, but snip it off and leave it in the fish where it will eventually dissolve. Better yet, if you really aren't going to keep fish, don't use live bait at all. Artificial lures, especially when paired with barbless hooks (now necessary in the Quetico – you can legally squash down the barb of a regular hook to comply) make releasing a fish unharmed a much simpler task.

If you remember nothing else from this chapter except that you should use small baits over rocky rubble, you'll take smallmouth. And once you tie into one of these testy little devils you'll always remember just how fun fishing can be. Smallmouth are a great fish to introduce new anglers to the sport of fishing. They are relatively easy to catch, they are great fun on a rod, and, if a fresh fish dinner is on your mind, fine eating as well.

A Mixed Bag

While walleyes, northern pike, lake trout and smallmouth bass are the most common and popular gamefish in the Canoe Country, they are by no means the only catchable fish present. Muskies are reported in a couple of lakes, introduced some years ago by man, though their actual presence today may be questionable -- except in East Pike Lake, where I've caught several of them. Largemouth bass, normally a fish thought of in connection with warm southern waters, can be found in a few lakes and provide some very fine fishing – in fact, they are the only native bass to the region. Lake whitefish, commonly thought of as a commercially harvested species, thrive in some of the large walleye and lake trout lakes. When the mayfly hatch is on they are great sport on a flyrod. There are also sauger (a near relative to walleye), black crappies, and even sturgeon for those who want something a bit different on the end of their line.

Some of the best BWCAW fishing opportunities for species other than walleye, northern pike and smallmouth bass are those of the stream trout lakes. Lakes, usually small, that the Minnesota DNR deem suitable for trout have been "reclaimed" and stocked with brook trout. These lakes formerly harbored either no fish, or populations of stunted fish. The DNR, after identifying these lakes, began poisoning them out using a fish toxicant, and stocking them with a variety of stream trout. It has been one of their best programs.

When this book first came out, there were a fair number of stream trout lakes that contained rainbow and brown trout, or splake. However, because the Boundary Waters is a federal wilderness, and these areas are set aside to preserve native species, in 1989 the DNR and the U.S. Forest Service reached an agreement to limit stockings to brook trout, which although native to the surrounding watershed, were never natively found in any Boundary Waters lakes. There are a couple of exceptions – if a lake was stocked with rainbow trout or splake (a cross between lake trout and brook trout) before the BWCAW was declared a wilderness (1964), or expanded in 1978, those stockings could continue. There aren't

many -- you'll find just a couple of lakes that can still be stocked with rainbow trout or splake. Ontario does not stock stream trout of any species in the Quetico, nor are there any native brook trout populations.

These stream trout lakes provide a fishery that was otherwise unavailable in the BWCAW. If you are passing near one of them it, could be worth the detour to give it a try. The reclaimed trout lakes are generally not on heavily used canoe routes and are more often a dead end location.

If you have never caught a brook trout from these cold northern waters, if you have never seen the jewels on their sides, if you have never tasted one fried to a golden crisp, well then some would say you just haven't lived.

These little trout lakes have something special about them besides the fish. With the mist of a cool morning rising from its surface, a more primordial scene could not be found. Even the fact that the very reason you are there is because the lake had been tampered with by man takes away none of its wildness. It just goes to show that sometimes mankind can do things right and actually work with, instead of against, nature.

When a hatch is on the best way to fish brook trout lakes is with flies. Fishing to rising trout with hardware or bait is commonly a fruitless experience. The fish are keyed in on insects at this point and the best lure or juiciest worm will seldom draw a strike. The rest of the time, however, brookies will take lures or bait. A word here about bait: there is a restriction on the use of live bait in managed stream trout lakes. You cannot use minnows. Thoughtless anglers have ruined many good lakes by dumping leftover minnows into the water. You can, however, use leeches and worms, and both of these are effective when fished virtually the same way you would for smallmouth.

The equipment you have with you will suffice for a short stint of fishing in these lakes. The smallest lures in your tackle box will be the ones that will produce the best. Tiny spinners, such as the Mepps and Vibrax, are very good for trout and your smaller plugs and lake trout spoons will produce as well. There are a couple of things that you might want to consider doing that may be different than the rest of your BWCAW fishing. Trout are among the spookiest of fish and a light line is a must. If you have six pound test line on your reel, you can probably get by, but anything heavier will drastically cut down on your fishing success. The best thing to do is carry a spool for your reel containing four pound line or at the very least, tie in a leader of four pound. Carrying a light line like this, whether on a spare reel spool or on a leader wheel, is a good idea for much of your fishing. There are times that even walleyes and smallmouth can be spooky and require that you use light line.

Brook trout seem to like lures that are basically silver or gold. A couple of very good combinations are silver and blue or gold and orange. The silver and gold colors should make up the bulk of the lure's color. A spoon I've used with great luck is a gold and orange Krocodile. This one is also a very good spoon for lake trout and splake and is always in my kit.

The real trick in catching stream trout in lakes is not so much what they will bite on, but where the devil to find them. Since they are stream fish, they do not seem to relate to lake bottom structure the way other fish do.

In fact, they don't pay much attention to it at all. What they are most interested in is the water temperature, a factor that is critical. Wherever the right temperature is, that is where you will find the fish. It may be on the bottom, close to shore or someplace midway between the surface and the bottom. The second thing that interests them is eating. All trout feed extensively on insects during their early years. As they get larger they eat a lot more minnows and sometimes each other. Big trout are very cannibalistic.

When the combination of temperature and food is right, the fishing will be good. How does one determine this? It takes a lot of trial and error. Again, trolling may be your best bet. By experimenting with location and depth one should be able to catch fish.

In the spring and early summer the brook trout can and will be scattered because the water temperature is often very nearly a constant cool throughout. It does make them a little harder to find but, on the angler's side, almost all of these lakes are small, some even tiny, and it does not take a lot of effort to cover them thoroughly.

Later in the summer, as the waters warm up, the stream trout can be a bit more concentrated. If you've ever looked at the makeup of some of these lakes you will find that many of them are not very deep. Yet trout must have cool to cold water, their upper temperature range peaking out at a few degrees over seventy. Knowing that the lakes are fairly shallow, and that the DNR wouldn't put trout in lakes that were unsuitable, means that there must be some way of keeping the lakes cold in the summer. I have found that in many cases these lakes are kept cold by springs, often located in the deepest holes in the lake. At times when the rest of the lake has warmed up substantially, trout really crowd into these spring holes. The result is some very good fishing.

Perhaps the most interesting way to fish stream trout in lakes is by fly fishing. Even when the weather gets hot the trout will move into the shallows at dawn and dusk to take advantage of the insect hatches. If you are a devotee of the fly, I would recommend you pack your fly rod when heading into these lakes. The hatches are spread throughout the summer and mirror those of the rest of the Midwest, although they are usually a couple of weeks later being this far north. A selection of standard dry flies that work at home will work here and streamers and nymphs produce when the fish are not feeding on the surface.

A floating line for the dries and a sink-tip line for the streamers and nymphs are all that you need. Since even the spring holes in some of the trout lakes are only twenty feet deepm a fly angler with a sink-tip or sink-head fly line can probe them effectively. Brightly colored streamers and nondescript nymphs should be in your fly box. Try trolling streamers and drifting with nymphs. When trolling for trout with hardware go slowly, slower yet with flies.

Whatever your means of fishing the stream trout lakes, I'm sure you will find it an interesting and rewarding experience.

A few lakes in the Boundary Waters and Quetico contain what are generally considered warm water species and are uncommon to this area, such as panfish and largemouth bass.

The largemouth I've encountered in this wilderness behave the same as they do elsewhere. They are much fonder of warm water and weedy areas than are their cousin the smallmouth. They are not fussy about the bottom and you can find them in mucky, warm back bays where no self respecting smallmouth would be caught dead. While they don't reach the size of southern bass, they average a nice size in some lakes and seldom are either overpopulated or stunted. Because the water is cooler than what would be considered ideal largemouth bass temperatures, they never really get to be monsters. The cool, clean waters of the northland make them better eating bass than some I've encountered and they might surprise some who may never have liked to eat bass.

The equipment that you have for walleye and smallmouth bass fishing will do just fine. Try top water lures along shore or use bait or lures near weed beds and stumps. Serious largemouth bass anglers will want to try their Texas-rigged plastic worms. The way to create a Texas rig is to insert the hook into the plastic and run it into the worm about one quarter of an inch. Slide the worm all the way to the eye of the hook, then turn the barb of the hook toward the worm and bury it (making it weedless). A cone shaped sinker is placed on your line first, which then runs down to the hook eye. This is a deadly lure for largemouth, and also can be effective on smallmouth and walleyes at times. Be sure that the worm hangs straight or it will twist your line.

Cast this rig to bass cover, and let it sink with "controlled slack." A contradiction in terms, maybe, but what you are trying to achieve is to let the lure sink naturally, but not have so much slack in the line you can't feel the bass grab it as it sinks – which is when most of the strikes will occur.

If the rig falls to the bottom without a hit, let it sit for a few seconds before beginning your retrieve. There are two good methods for retrieving a Texas-rig. The first is to slowly lift the rod, then drop it, letting the luring settle back. Reel up the slack. Repeat. This is a slow methodical approach.

The second approach sometimes works well when largemouth are being finicky. Instead of slowly lifting the rod, this time try snapping it back quickly, using your wrist. You want the worm to jump three to four feet

up. Again, using "controlled slack" let it fall to the bottom again. Be prepared, as it is falling, for a strike.

I used to think it was a bit silly to venture onto these northern lakes looking for warm water species. No longer. Some fantastic largemouth fishing can be found, and, if you are a fan of panfish, you may well be surprised by the size and number of big bluegills to be found. In the lake index you'll find that bluegills receive their own designation (BG), since they tend to grow the largest of the panfish, and are more desirable both on the rod and in the pan. All the other panfish are listed as "SF" – for sunfish, usually green-eared sunfish, pumpkinseed, or hybrid sunfish.

Panfish – mostly bluegills – aren't uncommon in the Canoe Country. But they aren't spread throughout the lakes in which they are found. Remember that this far north, these lakes tend to be cool – even the ones that are relatively shallow. Look for back bays with lots of weeds and sandy or mucky bottoms when prospecting for panfish. If panfish are your "thing" back home, you'll recognize the water quickly. And the panfish will behave just as they do back home – very aggressively early in the season when they are on their spawning beds, and on the surface to small poppers in early summer before the water gets too warm. I tend to throw in a few small eighth ounce panfish jigs in my box when I know I'm going to be in an area where these fish are found. Jigging can be

very effective, as can small flies. In fact, given the choice, I'd rather use flies on panfish than any other technique, and not just because I enjoy fly fishing. Flies actually better imitate the small foods that these fish prefer. Wooly Worms fished slow beneath the surface are absolutely deadly. When bluegills are rising, they simply will not take anything but a small popper or dry fly.

A close cousin to the walleye, saugers can be found in several lakes in the Quetico. Fishing for saugers is nearly identical to angling for walleye, and they are often taken in the same locations. In fact, it is a pretty safe bet that quite a few anglers have caught saugers on canoe trips and didn't realize it, thinking they were small walleyes. You can tell a sauger from a walleye by examining the dorsal (top center) fin. Saugers have numerous black spots on this fin, walleyes don't.

I doubt that anyone ventures into the Canoe Country for saugers, but don't pass them up if you stumble upon some. The techniques described for walleye angling are identical to what you need to know for saugers. They are a fine sport fish, and excellent dinner fare.

What else might you encounter? Well, there are some lakes that have good numbers of crappies, though these fish, because they are often suspended in the water column, are difficult to locate, and difficult to fish. As a winter fishery, they are fantastic. As mentioned, muskies are rumored to be in a few lakes, but confirmed in only one. Rock bass are common, but are a pretty undesirable species, neither much fun to catch or good to eat. Eelpout (sometimes called lawyers, and a member of the cod family) are quite common in many lake trout lakes. They are a strange, eel-like primitive fish that are unpleasant to handle, but downright delicious to eat. If you're the adventurous type, you might just want to throw one in the pot. For good reason they are often called "poor man's lobster."

Whitefish are common, though not commonly caught. With an underslung jaw, these delicate fish most often feed on zooplankton. But they will often rise to take emerging insects such as mayflies. If, while a hatch occurs, you see fish rising in the middle of a lake rather than along the shore, they are most likely whitefish. If you're equipped to fish dry flies, give them a try. Whitefish are excellent table fare.

With a little careful planning, some scrutinizing of the information in this book and a willingness to go a bit out of your way, you can end up with a very diversified fishing trip into the Boundary Waters. The really nice thing about this country is that the rewards are seldom not worth the efforts.

Even if they don't result in more fish they are bound to leave you with fine memories and scenes of beauty. Fishing trip success is not always measured by the number of dead fish.

I Caught One -Now What?

Catching fish is fun, or at least is supposed to be if you don't take it too seriously. Most anglers are content to catch and release fish, keeping a few for meals along the way. There are a few who insist on packing out limits of fish, but those anglers are, fortunately, diminishing in number. Yes, these are lightly fished lakes (compared to boat accessible waters), but the fact remains that they are also fragile fisheries because the growing season is so short this far north. Fish take many years to mature to spawning age, and killing lots of big fish can harm the population. Lake trout, for instance, grow at less than a pound a year. If you catch a ten pound laker while canoeing the wilderness, it may be twenty years old!

That said, there is absolutely nothing wrong with keeping a few medium to small fish for meals. In fact, for many visitors, it is a ritual that they look forward to with great relish. All of the fish from the Canoe Country are mighty fine eating if properly cared for between the time they leave the water and enter your mouth. Environmentally, there is sense in eating locally. Rather than hauling in protein – meat, soy, or tuna fish – grown or harvested half a continent or world away with all the fossil fuel costs that implies, keeping and eating fish taken from the lake on which you're camped has far less impact on the planet. However, it is your responsibility to kill only what you need for a meal, which is often less than a legal limit, and return all other fish to the lake in good shape.

In this respect it is the duty of the angler to learn the proper handling of fish. It is a terrible waste to get back to camp and find the fish unsuitable to eat. We should also take care while releasing unwanted or not needed fish to insure their best chance of survival. No one will be there to watch you so in all these respects your own conscience must be your guide. It is sometimes a trademark of the species that mankind does not always treat his fellow creatures with the care and respect they deserve. You've gone to the trouble to catch a fish, now take the time to release or clean and cook it the right way.

Releasing fish unharmed requires two tools. One is a needle nose pliers and the other is wet hands. A lot of folks are afraid of touching fish and swing the fish into the canoe, letting it flop until it is quiet. They then rip the hooks out and flip the fish over the side. I don't know what they are doing fishing or what they could be thinking about, but it certainly isn't the welfare of the fish or the resource. With the wet hands and the pliers you can do it all while the fish is in the water without damaging it.

When you have brought a fish to the side of the canoe and have determined that you want to release it, you must act quickly and calmly. If the fish is hooked in the lips or the jaw, the hook plainly visible, take your needle nose pliers and grasp the hook as close to the point where it enters the flesh as you can. Then simply twist and shake until the hook comes free. All of this should be done while the fish is supported by the water. If you hoist the fish into the air, its own weight will keep the hook from slipping free, not to mention the fact that you may do damage to the internal organs. With lures with more than one set of hooks, be careful of hooking yourself.

If the fish is hooked on the inside of the mouth the process is the same, though a bit more difficult. Hooks that are plainly visible can be treated like those in the lips or jaw. If they are far enough back to make them hard to get at, you may have to handle the fish. This is where the wet hands come in. All fish secrete a mucous that coats their body and protects them from infections. If this is scraped off, whether by dry hands, dry landing nets or banging around in the canoe, the fish stands a good chance of not surviving once released.

A wet hand will affect this mucous much less severely than a dry one. To get at the hook in the mouth, slide your wet hand to the middle of the fish's belly, palm up. You can then lift the fish and turn it so you can see into its mouth to remove the hook. After doing so, release the fish gently. Never toss a fish into the water! Just set it back down. Be careful not to damage the gills by hitting them with the hooks or pliers. If the fish is very active and squirms around, you may have to apply a little more pressure. Don't do it on the belly but bring your hand up to the back, grasping the fish between the gill covers and the top fin in the firm, meaty area. Try not to stick your fingers in the gills.

Smallmouth and largemouth bass can be lifted into the canoe by firmly grasping their lower jaws between thumb and forefinger. Their teeth are small and pose no problem. This grasp paralyzes them for a time until you can remove the hooks. If the fish is to be released, do it quickly and while the fish is still partially in the water. All other fish can be handled by sliding your hand back to their midsection, again while they are still in the lake, and lifting slightly. At this point you can remove the hook or stick it on the stringer. Don't grab a fish by the eye sockets or gills if it is to be released or even if you want to keep it alive on the stringer as this will surely kill or blind the fish.

Fish hooked in the gills are usually goners. If the fish is hooked lightly and there is no bleeding, you may be able to let it go. Treat it just like you did for a fish hooked in the mouth, taking extra care not to tear the gills. Sometimes the hooks are near the rear of the gills. These are better removed by taking them out through the gill cover opening. Remove the leader or line from the lure and ease the lure out, hooks first, through the rear. If the fish bleeds after removal of the hooks, reduce it to your bag. It will not survive.

When using live bait it is not unusual to have a fish swallow the rig, hook, line and sinker as they say. Unless it is easily reached and lightly imbedded you are much better off to simply reach in and snip the line as close to the hook as possible. Don't be lazy or a cheapskate and try to save the hook. A wasted fish just isn't worth a hook. Tests have proven that the fish will survive with the hook left in, especially when the other option is a lot of probing and poking. The fish's own secretions will quickly dissolve the line and eventually the hook.

The key points to remember when releasing a fish are to handle it as little as possible, use wet hands if touching the fish is a must, be careful of the gills, and that it is better to leave a hook in than force it out. A fish whose gills are bleeding should not be released.

Releasing fish is made much easier if you use barbless hooks. Quetico now requires that all hooks be barbless (these can be barbed hooks with the barb flattened with your pliers), and it is a good idea to practice this in the Boundary Waters as well. A barbless hook slips out of the fish much more easily, and leaves a smaller wound.

CATCH AND RELEASE TIPS

-- *DON'T OVER-TIRE THE FISH; IF YOU KNOW YOU'RE GOING TO BE RELEASING FISH, GET THEM TO THE CANOE QUICKLY.*

-- *DON'T REMOVE THE FISH FROM THE WATER UNLESS NECESSARY.*

-- *IF YOU DO NEED TO HANDLE THE FISH, USE A WET HAND, AND BE SURE TO PROVIDE SUPPORT FOR ITS BODY.*

-- *A NEEDLE-NOSE PLIERS IS A MUST-HAVE TOOL!*

Over the years, I've also had the duty of removing hooks from other anglers. Believe me, that something that is no fun, and had they been using barbless hooks, it would have been easier on everyone. Flatten your barbs and save yourself and the fish some hassles.

If you decide to keep the fish you must take care of it as well. A fish that goes belly up alongside the canoe and floats around in the warm water will go bad quickly. Since the canoeing angler will seldom have a cooler in which to put fish, proper use of a stringer is the only alternative while still on the water.

Whether you use a cord stringer or the type with clips, it is important that it be long enough to allow the fish to get down into cooler water and under the shadow of your canoe. If you can, tie the stringer on the shady side of the canoe. This is more important on hot summer days than those chilly days of spring. The sun can quickly heat up the top layer of water and the additional stress to the fish will cause it to quickly succumb.

Never put the stringer in the fish's mouth and out its gill covering. You are much better off to impale it through one or both lips. If the fish is to be kept alive a long time it should be hooked through one lip only. In this manner the fish is free to open its mouth to breathe. Of course, big fish may require that the stringer be placed through both lips so he doesn't twist free. A large fish can put a lot of torque on the clip-on stringers and force the latch open. They have even been known to tear the clip free of the rest of the stringer. It is a matter of judgment whether or not to use both lips. As a general rule, one lip on smaller fish is enough and will keep them alive longer. The only time I put a stringer through both the upper and lower jaw is if we must paddle a fairly long distance back to camp. If you place the stringer through just one jaw, the speed of the canoe will actually force the fish's mouth open and force water through it at a rate that can cause it to drown. Yes, you can drown a fish.

Occasionally you may catch a fish at dusk and want to keep it overnight for breakfast. When attempting to keep fish alive overnight, add a length of rope to the stringer to allow the fish access to deeper water. The fewer fish per stringer, the longer they will stay alive and the less chance that they will tear free. Keep an eye out for snapping turtles; they have been known to devour fish left on a stringer. There is a much smaller chance of this happening if the fish is still very much alive and alert, and the stringer long enough to allow it to keep away from the turtle.

Fish that need to be transported, say across a portage, can be kept fresh in an old burlap sack. Leave the fish whole and put them in a completely soaked sack. The evaporation will keep the fish amazingly cool and also prevent flies from doing their thing. Keep it hung up while in camp so air can freely circulate about it, enhancing the evaporation process. Periodically wet down the bag.

Some may question how long a fish will remain fresh enough to be safe to eat. As long as the gills are still red or pink, the fish should be OK. Once the gills have turned a brown color, chances are you have waited too long before eating it. Another test is to press a finger into a meaty area. If it is very mushy, if your finger leaves an imprint that does not bounce back in a second or two, it may be unsuitable. When the gills still have some color, the flesh still fairly firm and its smell is fresh, go ahead and clean it. It should still make a mighty tasty meal. When it is possible, you are best off to keep the fish alive until it is time to clean it. A sharp rap with a stick or stone behind the eyes on the top of the skull will dispatch it quickly and humanely.

Occasionally we run across fish that have parasites living in or on them. For the most part this presents no problem and the fish will not only be safe to eat once cooked but also taste just fine.

Parasites may be found on the outside of a fish, in the internal organs or in the flesh. Those found in the internal organs present the smallest problem since these will be discarded with the offal. Try not to puncture the organs while cleaning the fish. Besides allowing parasites to possibly get onto the meat, it just isn't a good practice to allow all that yucky stuff to taint the edible parts.

Parasites on the outside will also not affect the fish's eating quality since most of the time the skin will be removed. While external parasites come in all shapes and types, they are most often found in the gills, eyes or under the scales. Again, they present not much of a problem as these areas will be discarded. One infection that should be avoided are fungal types. Easily recognized, they appear as a white cottony growth of fur or hair on the fish's back, belly and sides. While they are no threat to human safety if the fish is consumed, they impart a bad flavor.

Two other common parasites encountered by fishermen are known as ICH and black spot. ICH is a protozoan that appears as small white spots on the skin or gills. Once the fish is cleaned and skinned it is safe to eat. Black spot is also found on the skin and sometimes in the flesh. These small black cysts look like tiny black spots (hence the name!) on the skin or in the flesh. Fish with black spot are totally safe to eat once cooked, as this parasite impart no bad taste. They rather look like someone heavily peppered the fish while cooking and if you have squeamish members in your party, it is totally allowable to pass it off as such.

One parasite that can be of concern is the broadfish tapeworm. A larval form of tapeworm that can develop into an adult in humans, it is harmful if not killed. They are found most often in northern pike but are not uncommon in walleye, perch and eelpout. Broadfish tapeworms look like a white glistening worm about one to one and a half inches long. It is found in the muscle (flesh) of the fish.

In order to eliminate the danger of introducing this parasite into your own system the fish must be cooked at a temperature of one hundred forty degrees. Unless you consider yourself a campfire gourmet and prepare oriental or South American raw fish cuisine, such as seviche, your normal cooking procedure will render the parasite harmless. Should you be taking fish home with you it is important to know that freezing at zero degrees will also kill it. Cold smoking or pickling without cooking or freezing first may not kill the tapeworm. While not something to cause you to swear off eating fish, there have been a few individuals in this area who have been infected because they did not take the proper precautions.

Just the act of cleaning the fish will eliminate most of your concerns about parasites. More often than not it will be easier to cook the fish and better tasting if it is filleted. By filleting the fish you eliminate the bothersome bones and any "fishy" flavor that some object to. You also leave very little waste and the fillets will cook much more evenly and completely than a fish cut into steaks. The only possible exception to this are small trout which are delicious when cooked whole, sans gills and guts, or boiled fish steaks.

I don't want to spook you about parasites. They are rare. In all my years of angling in the Canoe Country, I can count on one hand the number of fish I've encountered that have had one of the above parasites. You should, however, watch for them.

Most of your camp recipes will call for fish fillets. If you are an experienced angler, most likely you already know how to fillet your

A canoe paddle makes a good surface for filleting fish. Always clean fish well away from any campsites.

catch. For those of you who have never tried it before, filleting is not difficult but does require practice and two accessories. One is the fillet knife and the other is a smooth, clean surface upon which to work.

Your fillet knife should be sharp, sharp, sharp! It must have a flexible blade tapering to a fine point of at least six inches. It is awful handy to have some means of sharpening the blade with you on your trip as you should sharpen it about every other fish. Fillet knives are easy to sharpen but for the same reason, dull pretty quickly. You will lend a new definition to the term butchering if you attempt to fillet a fish with a dull knife.

All fish can be filleted and most will be done in the same manner. Northern pike will require a slightly different process to eliminate the "Y" bones that they are noted for. The skin should be removed from all fish although some like to leave the skin on trout. This saves you the messy task of scaling and the skin, especially that of the bass, adds nothing to the flavor and often detracts from it. Lake trout scales are so tiny that if you decide to leave the skin on you'll not need to scale the fish first. There are a few campfire recipes that do require skin be left on – such as wrapping the fish or fillets in foil with vegetables and butter and roasting them in the coals. In these cases, go ahead and leave the skin on, but make sure you remove the scales on all species other than lake or brook trout. To scale fish, use the back of your knife and scrape the skin from tail to head (against the "grain" of the scales).

The other thing you will need to fillet the fish besides the knife is a smooth working area. The bottom of an overturned canoe works nicely as does a canoe paddle blade. Place either of these so that they are level and you are ready to begin.

I urge everyone to avoid cleaning fish in their campsite. It is a much better practice to paddle out to a rocky island, or down the shoreline a few hundred yards, and do the cleaning and filleting there. This is a bit of a messy task, and introducing fish slime, scales and blood to a campsite is a sure way of inviting pests. Flies will surely pester you and the next party to camp in that location, and bears are another potential visitor you don't want to attract. Please keep the campsites clean by filleting elsewhere!

These instructions are for the right handed individuals. Merely reverse them if you're a lefty.

While everyone probably has a slightly different variation on the process, here is the way I like to fillet fish. You'll note I fillet the first half without cutting through the rib bones, but on the second half I do. Because of the slant of the bones, I find it easy to remove the first fillet without slicing through the bones, but easier on the second filet to cut through the rib bones, then remove them afterwards. You may find that you like to do both fillets either by cutting around the rib bones, or by slicing through them, then removing them. Certainly, cutting through the rib bones is faster -- if you prefer this method, you can just skip ahead to the instructions for figures 8 and 9. However, slicing through the rib bones also quickly dulls your fillet knife, especially on bass and panfish.

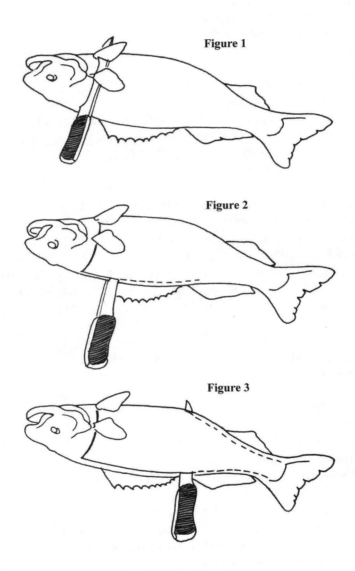

Figure 1

Figure 2

Figure 3

General Filleting

Figure 1. Start with the fish on its side, head to your left hand and its back facing you. Make your first cut behind the head and front fin, starting at the back and cutting down toward the belly. This first cut should go only as deep as the spine, which you will feel with the knife blade. Do not cut through the spine.

Figure 2. Now, with the blade turned parallel to the cleaning surface, cut toward the tail. The knife blade should be angled slightly downward to keep it sliding along the spine and the tip of the blade should be tickling the top of the rib cage, which is about half way down the fish's side. Continue cutting toward the tail until you reach the end of the fish's ribs, about two thirds of the way down its length or just in front of where the body begins to taper toward the tail.

Figure 3. When you reach this point push the tip of the knife through to the belly...

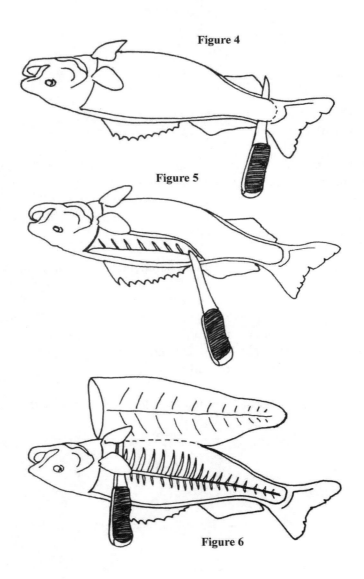

Figure 4

Figure 5

Figure 6

Figure 4 ...and continue back toward the tail with the blade still sliding along the spine. When you get to the tail, cut through the skin.

Figure 5. The meat is still attached to the ribs at this time so go back up to them. Grab the flesh along the back above where the ribs are and gently lift up, as if you were trying to open a book. While lifting, cut the flesh away from the rib cage with light strokes. This should be done with the tip of the blade and care should be taken not to angle it too much. The meat here is thin and easily cut through or wasted so keep that blade against the rib bones.

Figure 6. Once you have sliced the meat away from the ribs, open the fillet up and slice away at the belly line back toward where you already cut through. By removing the fillet from the ribs in this manner, there's less wasted meat, and less wear and tear on your knife's edge.

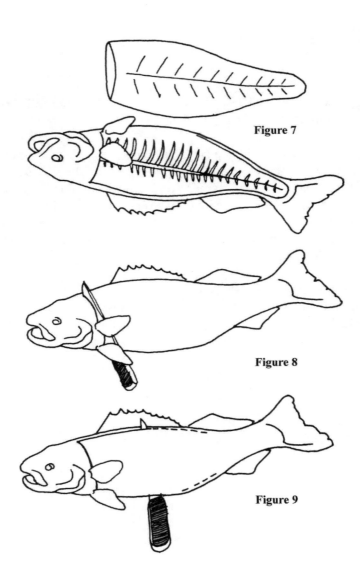

Figure 7

Figure 8

Figure 9

Figure 7. You now have one boneless, though unskinned, fillet. Set it aside for now.

Figure 8. Now for side two. Flip the fish over, head still toward your left, and make the same first cut as before, behind the head and front fin stopping at the spine.

Figure 9. Turning the blade edge toward the tail, the knife fully extended from back to belly, cut along the spine back to the tail. This time, you will cut right through the rib cage so you may have to apply a little force. If you prefer, you can fillet both sides of the fish in this manner, cutting through the ribs.

Figure 10

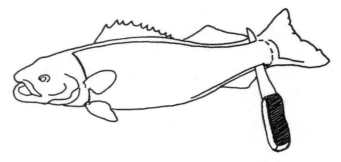

Figure 11

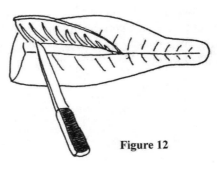

Figure 12

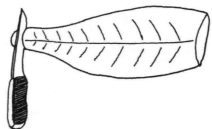

Figure 10. After cutting through the ribs continue to the tail and slice through the skin. You will end up with a fillet with the skin and ribs still attached.

Figure 11. Lay the last fillet skin side down with the top of the rib cage toward you. Using the tip of your knife, begin to cut away the ribs at what was the head end. It helps to lift the bones with the fingers of your free hand while sliding the knife between the ribs and the flesh. Again, be careful here as the meat is thin. Because the ribs slant backwards to the tail it is easier to work in that direction. Keep the knife at a slight upward angle. Once done with that you should have two boneless fillets.

Figure 12. All that is left to do is skin the fillets. Starting at the tail, pinch the very tip to the work surface with your fingertips. Take the knife blade and starting as close as you can to your fingertips, cut down ever so slightly until you reach the skin. Be careful not to cut through the skin.

Figure 13

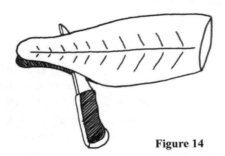

Figure 14

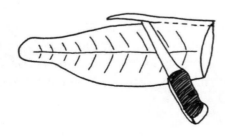

Figure 13. Now just turn the knife blade flat and slide it up the fillet toward the far end. The blade must be maintained at a very small downward angle so you do not leave any meat attached to the skin. It sometimes helps to use a slight sawing action as you work your way along. This task requires that you use both a little force and at the same time great care. Turn the knife too much one way or the other and you either cut through the skin or the meat. Thin-skinned fish like the trout require more caution than do walleyes or bass.

Figure 14. Fillets should be trimmed of belly meat (the white stuff at the bottom that gives off a foul flavor) and any pieces of fins before it is skinned.

That's about it. After rinsing them with clean water, you should have two nice boneless fillets all ready for the frying pan. Fillets from larger fish should be cut into smaller pieces for cooking.

Northern Pike Filleting

If you are lucky enough to land a big northern pike and have a hankering for a fish dinner, you should find it suitable dinner fare. One can still fillet pike, regardless of the "Y" bones that inhabit the fleshy sides, and end up with boneless portions. It requires that you modify the procedure just outlined. Let's go through it step by step.

Figure 1. To fillet a northern pike, lay it on its belly, not its side. If you are right handed its head should face toward your left. Hold it by the head and make your fillet cut just behind the skull, down until you hit the spine. Do not cut through the spine. Now turn the blade toward the tail and slide it along the backbone until you get to the back fin which is set far back on a pike's body. At that point cut upwards and remove the first fillet.

Figure 2. Turn the fish on its side now and look toward the tail just below the point where you ended the top cut is where you will make the next incision. This area of a pike does not contain "Y" bones so its removal is straightforward and similar to what we've discussed for other fish. Cut down to the backbone at a point just in front of the dorsal fin. When you reach the spine, do not cut through but turn the blade toward the tail. Slide the knife along the spine and slice through the skin at the tail just like you would for any species. Flip the fish over and do this same step on the other side. You should now have three fillets.

Figure 3. Now for the fun part. On both sides of the fish make a cut just behind the head stopping at the backbone, just as you did in step one for the other species.

Figure 4. Now put the pike back up on its belly. Looking down you should see the spine and a row of small bones running parallel on either side. If you can't see them, run your fingertip along the flesh and you will feel them. Take the very tip of your knife and insert it on the outside of one of these rows. Cut along this row back toward the tail with the tip of the knife angling slightly toward the center of the fish. Remember, these bones are not called "Y" bones for nothing. You are trying to run the

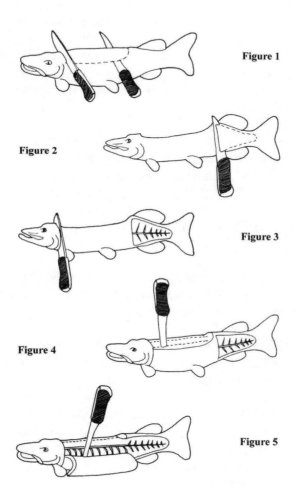

Figure 1

Figure 2

Figure 3

Figure 4

Figure 5

knife along the outside edge of one of the arms of the "Y" while at the same time while working to the tail.

Figure 5. After you've cut a little way down toward the belly you can gently begin to peel the flesh away while cutting. Soon you will reach the outside of the ribs. Using your knife tip follow the ribs down toward the belly and back toward the tail. When you've reached both the bottom and the back edge of the ribs you can cut the fillet away from the carcass. Repeat this procedure on the other side and you should end up with a total of five fillets.

These can then be skinned as you would any fillet although that top cut fillet may be a bit difficult because of its rounded shape. By following the knife blade closely with your hand and forcing the skin flat as you separate it from the flesh (the fish's, not your hand's) you should be able to remove the skin in one piece. If you have problems with this step, first swear (it helps relieve tension) then scale this piece and cook with the skin on.

With a little practice and some patience you should be able to master these techniques. Filleted fish are much better eating, quicker cooking and less of a mess than fish merely gutted, gilled and steaked.

Now that you're done cleaning the fish, and before you sit down to enjoy the fine meal those fillets will make, you are faced with the task of properly disposing of the carcass and entrails.

Hopefully you've taken my advice and filleted the fish well away from camp. If you did do it in camp, for goodness sake, don't throw the remains in the water off your campsite. Most of the time it will lay there on the bottom looking back up at you and every other camper who comes along for many weeks.

There is some debate on what to do with these remains. For instance, the U.S. Forest Service has wavered over the years between telling you to bury the carcass, or to place it on an exposed surface near the water's edge (well away from camp) for scavengers. Currently, the Forest Service tells you to bury the carcass. The folks at Quetico have been more consistent. They have long advocated the latter approach. The pros and cons of these methods are obvious. Burying the carcass on land, if not done a long way from camp, can lead to large scavengers (bears) digging it up. Encouraging bears to visit a lake that has campsites isn't a good thing! Placing the carcass on the water's edge for scavengers such as gulls and eagles puts "energy" into the land-based system. In other words, frequent meals of fish remains may encourage increased reproduction of gulls and other scavengers.

A good friend of mine who is a fisheries biologist has long told me that the best thing – ecologically speaking – would be to put the remains in the water. Fish die every day in lakes, he said, and the system is designed to recycle that energy back into the lake. That makes a lot of sense to me, as long as the remains are not put in the water near any campsites. The problem is that it is illegal to dispose of fish remains in lakes. Those rules, written after anglers would return to a boat launch site, clean their fish there, and make a cumulative mess over the course of a fishing season, make sense too. In the wilderness, though, these laws make little sense, and at one time the Forest Service even considered asking the Minnesota Legislature to exempt the Boundary Waters from this law.

Since I'm not advocating that you break any laws, you'll have to decide which method to use on your own.

Whatever method you use to dispose of fish remains, do so in a manner that will be unobtrusive to other visitors to the wilderness. Anglers often get labeled as slobs. When other wilderness users find a rotting walleye carcass in their drinking water in front of camp, you can hardly blame them for making that accusation. Take care to leave your campsite clean and free of such things as fish remains, shoreline rocks covered with dried blood and scales, lure packages and coils of used monofilament. Like practicing catch and release, such "no-trace" camping techniques prove that you really are concerned about our natural resources and leave you feeling good.

Cooking Fish

Few meals are as enjoyable as those cooked out of doors, whether over an open fire or atop your camp stove. We've all heard the adage that anything cooked and eaten outside tastes better. This is especially true when it comes to fish since it gives you the opportunity to eat truly fresh fish. Eaten "right off the hook" is about as fresh as you can get.

When cooking fish, it is important to remember not to overcook it. Fish loses much of its flavor, most of its moisture and nearly all of its nutritional value when overdone. There are no hard and fast rules as to how to tell when a fish is done, particularly when it has been filleted since one of the most common tests is to pull out a bone and see if the flesh sticks to it. Once filleted you should have no bones in your fish. Another rule says to cook until flaky (the fish, not the cook) but this often results in fish too well done, especially if the fish being prepared is one of the drier species which includes bass, walleye and specifically northern pike which is one of the driest of fresh water fish. Lake trout, because of its rich, oily texture can stand this test. Only time and experience can make the cook a good judge in this respect.

For camp cooking of fish, not many accessories or condiments will be needed. A frying pan or skillet is a must and a spatula will make the task easier. Those tiny frying pans that come with commercial camp cook kits

are practically useless. Better yet are aluminum fry pans of at least a
nine or ten inch diameter. These are available with fold down handles for

camping. It's nice if they are coated with a nonstick surface to make cleanup time easier. Skillets, the flat rectangular kind with a nonstick surface, are extremely handy when cooking for a larger party because of their big size. Foods in the out of doors cool quickly and it is nice to be able to cook enough for all at the same time, and a skillet allows you to cook two foods or plenty of fish for all. You may need two cook stoves under the skillet to heat its entire surface evenly. One disadvantage of skillets is that they don't have much of a "lip" or rim around them, so they don't hold much oil.

I actually prefer to cook fish over a wood fire. If you are in the Quetico, you can customize your fire pit to insure that your fire grate (you did bring one, didn't you?) is only six inches or so above the fire. All Boundary Waters campsites have a USFS firegrate in place, which is where fires must be built. These are often set so that the cooking surface is too far above the flame. That doesn't mean that you can't still cook on them. In cases like this, I usually find some large, flat rocks to place under the grate, and build the fire on them.

MINIMUM IMPACT TIPS

-- *KEEP A CLEAN CAMP TO AVOID BEAR PROBLEMS AND REDUCE ANNOYING INSECTS.*

-- *ALWAYS CLEAN FISH WELL AWAY FROM CAMP.*

-- *USE ONLY DEAD, DOWNED WOOD FOR CAMPFIRES. DON'T STRIP BIRCH BARK FROM UPRIGHT TREES.*

-- *CLEAN DISHES (AND YOURSELF!) AT LEAST 50 FEET AWAY FROM THE WATER.*

-- *FOOD LEFT-OVERS SHOULD BE BURNED OR BURY THEM FAR FROM CAMP.*

-- *PACK OUT NOT ONLY YOUR OWN TRASH, BUT TRASH YOU MAY HAVE FOUND ALONG THE WAY.*

Have a ready selection of a variety of sizes of wood on hand. What kind of wood? Some folks are fussy about the kind of firewood they use, but I have only one criteria -- it must be dry. Please collect only downed, dead wood, and for goodness sake, never leave a campfire unattended.

Once you have a good fire going, let it die down to a low flame with good coals, set the frying pan filled with oil on the grate, and allow the oil to get hot. Once you start cooking, the oil will cool down as the fillets are added. In order to quickly boost the temperature, I add bunches of small branches, preferably from dead conifers with the needles still attached. You know how your Christmas tree gets dry, brittle and becomes a fire hazard after a couple of weeks? That's the kind of needle-bearing, dry twigs you're looking for when scavenging from dead, downed trees. A couple bunches of these, tossed on the coals along with a few thumb-sized pieces of wood, quickly brings the oil back to the right temperature.

You'll need some vegetable oil in which to cook the fish. Unless you're putting your food in some kind of rigid pack, I'd repackage your oil into a Lexan water bottle, because the plastic bottles in which the oil comes can easily be punctured, leaving your food pack a mess. Once the heated oil begins to show a few bubbles on the bottom of the pan, it is ready to go. If you put the fish in too soon, it will just soak up a lot of oil and be greasy. That's also why it is important to keep adding a few twigs to the fire -- to keep the oil hot enough to fry the fish, not soak them. Hot, but not smoking! The deeper the oil in the pan, the more the fish will be deep fried. To simply fry, you'll want about a quarter of an inch of fat in the bottom of the pan. To deep fry, it should nearly, if not completely, cover the fillet.

Salt and pepper, as well as any other spices your little heart desires, should be taken along on the trip. They are light, use up little space, but add something special to your camp cuisine. A nice container for storing spices are those little plastic canisters in which 35mm film is packaged. Snap on lids with shaker tops are available from outfitters and mail order houses to make these canisters perfect for camping. With the advent of digital photography, these handy little containers are getting harder to find, but a visit to your local camera shop should provide you with what you need. They generally give them away.

About the only other supplies you need for cooking fish in camp are premixed dry fish batter, cornmeal or cornflake crumbs. You need not bring all of these, just your favorite. Each is used for coating the fillets, all are good, and which one to use is strictly a matter of personal preference. Just rinse the fillets, and while still damp, put them in a zip-lock bag with the dry batter. Shake to coat, and then remove the fillets as needed, and place them carefully into the oil. Be careful of grease spatters. You can get easily -- and painfully -- burned. A pair of tongs are nice for placing the fillets into the pan, and can be used for pulling them out, or flipping them.

Total cooking time for both sides will be somewhat less than ten minutes unless the fillets are over an inch thick. Thin fillets cook more quickly and generally taste better than thick ones. If the fish you filleted is a large one, and the filets thick, you might want to consider slicing them lengthwise into thinner pieces.

When the fillets have turned a crisp brown, serve. Keep an eye on your party member who is wolfing his serving down. Chances are he has his eye on not only his second piece but yours as well. You must be assertive here. Place yourself between him and the frying pan, even eat standing if you must. These degenerate fillet thieves deserve no quarter.

The oil can be re-used after it cools. If you're fussy, you can strain the bits of batter from it by using a piece of cheese cloth. The nice thing about cooking on wood is that, if you're not going to re-use the oil, you can pour it on the fire and burn it up. Be careful, as the flames can shoot quite high.

If you spent a bit of time on a stream trout lake you may have caught a few pan sized trout. Not many fish can compare to the delicate flavor of brook trout when cooked to a golden crisp.

Here is a time honored way to cook small trout:

- salt and pepper
- fresh trout, gutted and gilled but with head and tail left on
- some flour, cornmeal or cornflake crumbs
- butter or oil

Simply salt and pepper both the inside and outside of the fish, then coat the trout by rolling it in your choice of coating mix. Put the butter or oil in a pan that is over a medium heat. Low to medium heat will allow you to cook the trout slowly and brown it as well. Depending on the size of the fish the entire cooking time will run about fifteen to twenty minutes.

Once the coating mix has set on one side, flip the trout over gently. Brown the other side. Make sure it doesn't burn to the pan. It will require about ten minutes of slow cooking on each side to brown them to perfection.

When they are thoroughly browned, serve. Be careful not to break the fish into chunks. To eat, just remove the small fins by giving them a light tug. Leave the head and tail on to serve as handles and eat right off the bones, corn on the cob style.

Another method of preparing small trout whole, sans gills and guts, is wrapped in tinfoil and place under coals. If you are one of those who carries fresh veggies on your canoe trips, dice up some carrots, onion, celery or what have you and stuff the fish after sprinkling them inside and out with salt and pepper. Wrap each one in a piece of foil and bake under coals for fifteen to twenty minutes. The U.S. Forest Service campfire grates are a hindrance here but if you clean out the mess left by previous campers you should have room to work under them. Don't build a fire outside of the designated spot. By the way, you can prepare the fish this way without vegetables.

About the only justifiable reason for preparing fish in a steaked form (gutted and cut into one to two inch wide slices from back to belly) is when used as poor man's lobster. Lake trout lend themselves particularly well to this method of cooking, as do eelpout. Because lake trout are an oily fish, this method renders them especially tasty as the oil is boiled away. You'll need a couple of things special for this recipe so if you plan a lake trout trip, make provisions for hauling them along. It's a simple method of cooking fish and here is what you'll need:

- lake trout, steaked (gutted, gilled, skin on, cut into one to two inch wide steaks)
- salt, about a palm full
- a bay leaf or two
- a half dozen peppercorns
- butter
- a dash of lemon juice (optional)
- a hunk of cheesecloth (optional)

Bring water to boil in as big a pot as you have. Throw in the salt, bay leaf and peppercorns. Sit back and swat flies for a few minutes until this comes back to a boil and stews for about five minutes. If you have cheesecloth, wrap the trout steaks in it and lower into the water. You do not need the cheesecloth but it will help to keep the steaks in one piece. If you have none, just be careful when removing the steaks. Continue to boil for about five to seven minutes or until the fish starts to turn white. While doing this step melt some butter in a pan and when melted, stir in lemon juice, if available. Remove the fish when done, discard the skin and dip the chunks into the butter as you would lobster. Enjoy. If the fish is done properly, it will fall easily off the bones. Contrary to old wive's tales, I've found that mature lake trout have better flavor than young ones, though they are oilier. This method is particularly nice for those larger fish.

I suspect that most of the time your fish dinner will be simply fried. Fine. It's hard to beat a shore lunch of golden, crispy fillets fried just so. All fish can be prepared this way but are slightly different in their requirements. For instance, you can leave the skin on trout but it should be removed on most other species. This is a must for bass whether largemouth or smallmouth. Bass improve dramatically in palatability when the skin is discarded before cooking and can compare favorably with walleye if this step is performed. Northern pike require less cooking time, or a lower temperature, so they do not dry out, though thorough cooking of pike is important to safeguard against tapeworms (northern pike are more prone to carrying tapeworms than most other species). Lake trout should cook a bit longer because of their oil content.

Simple things, well earned, are the best things in life. Your own effort put you into this wonderful backcountry and supplied you with dinner. Done properly, fresh fish dinners will not only be something fondly remembered once home again, but greatly anticipated when planning your next trip. By taking care of fish from the time they are landed, whether released or saved for dinner, you can insure better fishing years down the road or some mighty fine eating back at camp.

It brings the whole experience full circle.

Portaging The Permit Path

It used to be that if you were going to get confused on a canoe trip, it happened while charting a course through the maze of aptly named Crooked Lake, or while seeking some seldom-used portage in Quetico Provincial Park.

While those things still may lead to confusion, many visitors to the Canoe Country now find the trip through the permit maze just as confounding. There are also other rules, such as bait restrictions, watercraft and fishing licensing, and border crossing issues to be aware of.

Here's what you need to know about these rules and procedures before venturing out on your next visit to the Boundary Waters or Quetico.

BWCAW OR QUETICO?

The first step in securing the correct permits is to determine your destination. Are you going to the Quetico? To the Boundary Waters Canoe Area Wilderness (BWCAW)? Both on the same trip? Will the trip be overnight, or are you taking a day trip? The answers to those questions will begin the process of figuring out just which permits you'll need.

First and foremost, each party needs a permit whenever they enter either wilderness, and permits for the Boundary Waters can not be used in the Quetico, or the reverse. Visitors to the Quetico require a permit from the Ontario Ministry of Natural Resources, and visitors to the Boundary Waters require a different permit from the U.S. Forest Service (USFS). While the procedures for acquiring these permits from each source are much the same, they are distinctly separate permits. Each wilderness also requires a permit to enter each time you visit, whether or not your party is making a day trip or staying overnight. Keep in mind, however, that day-use permits and overnight permits are not the same thing.

BWCAW _AND_ QUETICO?

What if your trip takes you to both wilderness areas on a single canoe trip? The answer is, as you might suspect, that your party needs a permit from each source, but you don't need an overnight camping permit if you'll not be camping.

For instance, if the bulk of your trip will be in the Quetico, and you're just paddling or motoring through the Boundary Waters to your Quetico entry point (and not staying overnight in the BWCAW) you'll need a Boundary Waters day-use paddle or motor permit in addition to your Quetico Provincial Park overnight permit. However, if your route requires that you'll be staying overnight in each wilderness, then you'll need two separate overnight permits – one each for the BWCAW and Quetico.

In the case where your party will just be passing through the BWCAW on its way to the Quetico with no overnight stops on the U.S. side, you'll need two separate day-use permits – one for your trip in, and one on the way back out.

However, it is allowable for you to use your BWCAW overnight permit both before entering and after exiting the Quetico, even though you are technically entering the BWCAW twice. As an example, take the famous "Hunters Island" canoe route, which lies half within Quetico, and half along the international boundary shared by the BWCAW and Quetico. If you begin your canoe trip at Moose Lake (which is in the U.S.) with a BWCAW permit, then paddle northeast up the border, camping on the U.S. side before picking up your Quetico permit at Quetico's Cache Bay Ranger Station on Saganaga Lake, you'd still be able to use your BWCAW overnight permit for the last leg back down the international boundary (from Lac La Croix to Basswood Lake), and be able to legally camp within the Boundary Waters.

Finally, there is one other exception to the rule of "one permit per wilderness" and that's when you're traveling down the international border. When on this border route – for instance, while traveling the

Basswood River – thanks to an international treaty, visitors can use portages on either the U.S. (BWCAW) or Canadian (Quetico) side. You also can fudge a little while paddling down a shared lake, since the boundary hasn't been painted on the water. Both the Quetico authorities and the USFS do, however, frown upon straying too far from the boundary. How far? Who knows. But you may get into trouble if you only possess a BWCAW permit and Quetico wardens find you well into Crooked Lake's Gardner Bay or other similar obvious transgression. And you must camp only on the side of the border for which your permit is applicable – i.e., if you have a BWCAW permit only, then you must camp on the U.S. side of border lakes.

THE BWCAW PERMIT SYSTEM

OK. This concept is pretty simple – your party needs a permit each time you enter the BWCAW, whether for overnight or day trips, regardless if you travel on foot, by paddle, or by motor. In addition to overnight and day-use paddle permits, the BWCAW has two other permit categories that Quetico does not – overnight and day-use motor permits. In all cases, permits should be carried on your person so that they are available for inspection by Forest Service rangers. If it all seems a little confusing, remember that the system was set up by the Forest Service to remain as flexible as possible, while still protecting the resource and your experience. A "one-size" fits all solution may be simpler, but it also would restrict your options.

BWCAW Day-Use Permits

Any party entering the BWCAW, whether by foot, paddle, or motor, but not staying overnight, needs a day-use permit of some kind year round.

Day-use permits for paddlers, hikers, dogsledders and skiers are a relatively new thing. Unlike overnight permits which are finite in number, self-issued day-use permits are unlimited in number. Entry points have permits available for self-registration, although the Forest Service reports that some locations are sometimes vandalized (permits all destroyed), so

BWCAW FACTS

-- MAXIMUM PARTY SIZE OF NINE; NO MORE THAN FOUR WATERCRAFT.

-- PERMIT ALLOWS YOU TO ENTER ONLY AT THE PLACE AND ON THE DATE SPECIFIED.

-- A PERMIT DOES NOT RESERVE A CAMPSITE; YOU ARE FREE TO CHOSE YOUR OWN, BUT IT MUST BE A USFS DESIGNATED SITE THAT HAS BOTH A FIREGRATE AND LATRINE.

it is a good idea to stop at a Forest Service office or a cooperating business to obtain one. If you're a frequent visitor, you can even grab a handful and keep them for future use, or you can call the Forest Service, and they'll mail you a stack to use when you need them.

Day-use motor permits, where motor use is allowed by law, are a horse of another color. Required from May 1 through September 30, they are limited in number, specific to a particular entry point, and thus are harder to obtain. Although technically, day-use motor permits are available on a first-come, first-served basis, at popular motorized entry points, they are frequently spoken for months ahead. Like any overnight permit, day-use motor permits should be reserved in advance to insure one is available for the date you plan to use it.

Day-use motor permits differ from other limited number permits in that they are established by a weekly quota. That is, if you know you want to enter at Moose Lake sometime during a particular week in July, but want the flexibility of choosing a nice day, you can reserve a permit for that particular week. That permit is still good for only one day, but once you know when you'll be going, you can choose that day, and it will be time-stamped on the permit when you pick it up to insure it is only used on that day. If you're using a motor before May 1, or after September 30, you can enter using the self-issued day-use permit.

BWCAW Overnight Quota Permits

All overnight visits to the BWCAW between May 1 and September 30 (the "ice-free season") require an overnight permit – one permit per party – and the procedure is the same whether or not you'll be traveling on a motorized lake, in the paddle-only zones, or backpacking. Overnight quota permits of all types are limited in number, and the number available varies from entry point to entry point. Overnight visits from October through April still require an overnight permit, but visitors can use the same self-issuing permit used for non-motorized day trips. The "ice-free" overnight permits are limited in number as prescribed by entry point quotas. There are no limits on the "winter" overnight, self-issued permits.

Again, although technically available on a first-come, first-served basis, (available at any USFS office or from cooperating businesses) in order to obtain an "ice-free" season overnight permit, it is wise to reserve them in advance, especially if you've chosen a popular entry point, or are entering at a peak period (opening of fishing season, times near holiday weekends, or anytime in July and August).

A permit allows you to enter only at the specified entry point, and only on the specified date. A maximum of nine people in up to four watercraft may travel on one permit. Members of your party that need to depart earlier than the rest, *and that can get out in a day without camping*, can do so without the need of another permit. However, if some members that are joining your party are entering the BWCAW later – *and can reach you in one day without camping* – they need to obtain either a motorized or paddle day-use permit. In other words, if you'll be camped out overnight, you need an overnight permit. Holders of two permits may not travel or camp together unless they don't exceed the nine person limit – you cannot exceed the nine person limit at any time no matter how many permits you hold. And a group all on one permit must camp together – you can't take two campsites, and you must be camped with the holder of the permit (party leader).

Once you have your permit, and have entered the wilderness at your designated entry point, you are free to travel wherever you want, and stay at any designated campsite (denoted by fireplace and latrine). A permit does not guarantee you a campsite on any particular lake, nor does it restrict you to any location. You can also stay in the BWCAW as long as you wish, provided you don't camp in any one site for more than 14 days, or exit the wilderness. With the exception of using your overnight permit both before and after a trip through the Quetico, once you exit the BWCAW, that permit is no longer valid.

BWCAW – Reserving And Picking Up Quota Permits

Visitors to the BWCAW have four options for reserving the quota-based overnight (paddle, hiking, or motorized) permit, or day-use motor permits needed between May 1 and September 30. Applications for each season may be submitted by website, fax, or mail beginning December 1. All applications will be processed by lottery (regardless of method or order received) until mid-January. After that, they'll be process on a first come, first served basis. Phone reservations will be accepted beginning the first business day in February. At the time of this writing, a $12 nonrefundable reservation fee is required for each permit. If reserving an overnight permit, a $32 deposit will be collected regardless of group size. Example: A total of $44 will be collected for an overnight reservation or $12 for a day use motor. There is now also a per-person, per-trip fee for overnight visitors. Adults are charged $16 per trip; those under seventeen are charged $8 per trip. These fees may increase over time, so please double check when making a permit reservation. Reservations require the use of a credit card. Fees are paid up front, at the time of reserving.

When making a telephone reservation, you will be asked for the following information:

-- Entry point
-- Arrival date and estimated exit date
-- Trip leader's name, address, postal code and telephone number
-- Estimated number of people and watercraft
-- Permit issuing station (where you'll pick up the permit)
-- Method of payment (i.e. credit card number and expiry date)

You can call the BWCAW Reservation Center toll free at **877-550-6777 (TDD at 800-TDD-NRRS**); fax a permit reservation request to them at 518-844-9951; visit the reservation website at **www.recreation.gov** and use the secure server to obtain a permit; or write to them at PO Box 462, Ballston Spa, NY, 12020. You must contact Recreation.gov, at the sources above, to reserve or cancel a permit. However, you can always stop at a USFS office or cooperating business and obtain a permit without reserving one, if any are still available.

However you reserve the quota permit, if one is available for your chosen entry point and date, the party leader will receive a confirmation letter or email. That confirmation reply is not your permit. The party leader (named in the permit) must pick up the permit at a Forest Service office, or from a cooperator. When you reserve the permit, you will be asked where you want to pick it up. The permit will be issued only to the party leader or a designated alternate (information you must provide when you reserve the permit). A photo ID is required to pick up the permit. You can pick the permit up only on the day of entry, or on the day before.

Bring the confirmation letter (print out the email reply) with you when you pick up the permit. If your party size has changed since the time you reserved your permit, that's fine (up to the maximum party size of nine, of course). Adjustments will be made when you pick up your permit. Allow time to view a short video on minimum impact camping practices

and take a quiz on BWCAW rules and regulations. To cancel your permit, call the BWCAW Reservation Center.

Minnesota Hunting, Fishing, and Watercraft Licenses

These aren't really Boundary Waters (USFS) regulations, but you still need to take note of them. Both hunting and fishing are allowed, subject to season and bag limits, in the BWCAW, and you'll need the appropriate valid Minnesota license and trout stamps to do them. These licenses are available at just about any bait shop or outfitter. Minnesota also requires boats, canoes, and kayaks to be licensed. If your watercraft is licensed in another state, that license will suffice. If your state does not require a canoe or kayak to be registered, you must either register it in your state as a motorized craft or license it in Minnesota. They can be registered at the DNR License Center, 500 Lafayette Road, Box 26, St. Paul, MN 55155-4026, phone: **651-296-2316**, or at any county registrar's office.

QUETICO PROVINCIAL PARK PERMIT SYSTEM

Procedures for obtaining a Quetico Provincial Park permit are very similar to those for the BWCAW, although obviously, you must go to a different source. There are two major differences. While BWCAW permits are picked up outside the area, at USFS offices or cooperators, Quetico permits are picked up at the entry point ranger stations, which are located in or on the edge of the park. Additionally, motor use is not allowed within Quetico, except for guides of the First Nation People of Lac La Croix, and so there are no public motor permits of any type.

Quetico Day-Use Permits

Day-use permits aren't as frequently used for the Quetico, for it is much more of a destination park than is the BWCAW. However, they are required if entering by canoe or dogsled, and they are the same as the Daily Vehicle permit. If you are entering by foot (hiking in the summer, showshoes or skis in the winter) no day-use permit is required. They are available at all entry point ranger stations and Quetico Park headquarters during the ice-free season. During the fall, winter and spring, you can self-register (and pay) at any of the ranger stations.

Quetico Overnight Permits

Like the BWCAW, if you're staying overnight in Quetico at any time of the year, you need an overnight permit. Permits for the ice-free season are based on quotas, and should be reserved. In the "off season" you can self register at ranger stations.

Although these quota permits are available on a first-come, first-served basis, they are even harder to obtain than BWCAW permits, since Quetico allows even fewer people to enter. Anyone planning a trip to the Quetico should reserve a permit well in advance.

An overnight permit allows up to nine people to enter on the date and at the entry point specified. Larger groups must have additional permits and must travel and camp separately. Ranger station operation hours during the summer season are from 8:30 a.m. to 4:15 p.m. Permits must be carried on you at all times. Since some of the southern ranger stations are rather remote, and require water travel to get there, park authorities will make reasonable allowances for delays caused by high winds or other dangerous weather. Permits for entry points controlled by Beaverhouse (also water-based), Atikokan or Dawson Trail ranger stations can be picked up at any one of these stations.

The "ice free" operating season is usually mid-May through the first week in September. Check with Ontario Parks to make sure.

Separate reservations and permits are required if your party plans to split up for the purpose of camping, or if someone in your group is entering after or leaving before the rest of your party.

Quetico Permit Reservations and Fees

Quetico Park permit reservations, cancellations, and changes are handled via phone, toll free, at 888-668-7275. This service is available 16 hours a day, seven days a week, 363 days a year. They have also instituted a new park information phone number, where a recorded message will provide you with up to date information on fire conditions, water levels and other details you should know before your trip: 807-597-4602. This is not a toll free number. Quetico permits, except for campground reservations (on the periphery of the park) cannot, at the time of this writing, be made via the internet. For general information on the park, call 807-597-2735.

When calling, you need to know your entry point, departure date, and will be asked for a group leader's name and a credit card for the confirmation and a deposit. Unlike the BWCAW which charges a flat-rate per-trip, per-person user fee, Quetico charges a per-person, per-night user fee, and the fees vary by entry point.

If you are a U.S. citizen and entering from the U.S. side – Cache Bay and Prairie Portage – the current rate is $19.80 (Canadian) per adult, per night, while those under 17 get by for $7.90 per night. If you are entering from Lac La Croix, the rates are $15.85 and $5.90. Non-Canadians entering from the north – Beaverhouse, Nym, etc. – the rates are $13.85 per night for adults, $5.90 for youth. The variety of rates reflects the

additional cost of maintaining ranger stations on the U.S. – Canadian border. Quetico collects $100 of this fee up front at the time you reserve the permit. Penalties for cancellation increase the nearer you get to the date of permit issuance. Penalties for "no shows" can be substantial. As noted with the BWCAW permits, these fee amount tend to change over time, so please double check before making a reservation.

The remainder of your overnight camping fees are paid when you pick up your permit at your entry point ranger station. It is strongly advised that you use a credit card to pay these fees to avoid problems with currency rates. Personal checks are not accepted. You can also purchase a fishing license at the ranger station.

Canada Customs and Ontario Regulations

> ## QUETICO FACTS
>
> *-- MAXIMUM PARTY SIZE OF NINE.*
>
> *-- PERMIT ALLOWS YOU TO ENTER ONLY AT THE PLACE AND ON THE DATE SPECIFIED.*
>
> *-- A PERMIT DOES NOT RESERVE A CAMPSITE; YOU ARE FREE TO CHOSE YOUR OWN. THERE ARE NO DESIGNATED CAMPSITES IN THE QUETICO.*
>
> *-- IF YOU ARE ENTERING BY PADDLE FROM THE SOUTH, YOU MUST HAVE A REMOTE AREA BORDER CROSSING PERMIT IN ADDITION TO YOUR QUETICO PERMIT.*

Another big difference between the BWCAW and the Quetico is that – to state the obvious – Quetico is in Canada. That means you'll be entering a foreign country, and that you'll need to go through Canada Customs station or obtain a CANPASS Remote Area Border Crossing (RABC) permit. Even in this post 9-11 era, we are still able to obtain this permit.

If you're driving to one of the northern entry points, you will clear Canada Customs at the highway border crossing, so won't need this permit. You must, however, have identification proving your citizenship, plus a second piece of ID. You should also have vaccination certificates for any animals with you (tags do not suffice). There no longer is any duty charged for bringing in foods. Since 2009, visitors to Canada need to have a passport.

If you're entering from the U.S. via Prairie Portage, Lac La Croix, or Cache Bay ranger stations, you must obtain a RABC permit from Canada Customs.

A CANPASS RABC permit allows the holder, and his or her spouse and dependant children, to enter on one permit. That means a family can all get by with one RABC permit, but if you have a party of four adults, you will need four separate permits. These permits are available to U.S. citizens or registered U.S. aliens. The cost is $30.00 Canadian, and it takes up to six weeks to process by mail, so plan to obtain this well in advance of departure. Use a VISA or Mastercard – checks are not accepted. You must provide proof of U.S. citizenship (a driver's license will not suffice), such as a copy of your birth certificate.

To obtain a RABC application form, write or call Canada Border Services Agency, CANPASS RABC Processing Centre, 201 North May Street, Floor 1, Thunder Bay, Ontario, Canada P9A 1H1; 807-274-9780.

Ontario does not require canoe registration, so you'll not have to worry about whether you canoe is licensed. You will, however, need to have a fishing license (hunting is not allowed in Quetico) and these can be obtained at any ranger station at the time you pick up your permit. Credit cards are accepted. For those of you who are only going to keep a few fish for meals, Ontario offers a conservation license at a reduced fee. Bag limits are smaller than the regular license, but still adequate to provide for a meal.

No live, preserved or organic baits are allowed in Quetico Provincial Park.

*****

There you have it. It isn't as easy as it used to be, that's for sure. The good news is, though, that all of these steps are taken before you depart, and once in the wilderness, you are free to enjoy its magnificence. The rules are there to protect your experience and the Canoe Country itself.

Many would argue that they are a small price to pay.

The Lakes Index

I first wrote this book in 1984, and it has been in print since that time. One of the things I long believed was that while equipment, techniques, and even rules and regulations would change over time, the lake information would not.

I was wrong.

If you have an earlier version of this book, you may be surprised to see many changes in the lake index. The first time I compiled this data, which included only Boundary Waters lakes in the first printings, I had to travel to each northern Minnesota Department of Natural Resource (DNR) office and paw through their file cabinets to extract the information. Today, that information is available on-line at their website (look for the "Lake Finder" link).

Having that information on-line today means I was able to check every lake in the index against their records – a long and tedious task! However, doing so allowed me to update many things, and I was surprised to find I was making changes to nearly every entry. Many of those changes were relatively minor things, such as lake acreage, which almost always went down. No, the lakes haven't shrunk due to global climate change (yet), but using aerial photos and computers, the agency was able to more accurately measure surface acreage.

In addition, some lakes that had never been surveyed have finally been visited by DNR field crews in the last twenty-five years. This has provided accurate information on the fish present in those lakes that formerly, if I listed it at all, was provided only by second hand reports from angling friends or fishing guides.

Checking the on-line data also revealed that a fair number of lakes have had fish stocked since the first edition of this book. Today, there are several lakes with good walleye fishing, or fishable populations of lake trout, thanks to these introductory stockings by the DNR.

Smallmouth bass, which aren't even native to the Canoe Country but were stocked initially be early fishing guides because they were easy for their clients to catch, are now listed in many more lakes than in the original book because they have relentlessly expanded their range. If two bodies of water are connected by a creek or stream, it seems inevitable that if one has smallmouth bass, the other will have them eventually. I don't even pretend to make the claim that the smallmouth information is up to date. I suspect that they are in many more lakes than noted here, especially in the Quetico where there are more interconnecting waterways. Smallmouth are quite the explorers, and continue their march across the Canoe Country.

You'll note some differences between the index for the Boundary Waters lakes and those found in the Quetico. The Minnesota DNR takes a more active role in inventorying and managing the lakes on their side of the border than does the Ontario Ministry of Natural Resources (MNR) on their side. That's understandable on two levels. First, the lakes in the Boundary Waters receive heavier fishing pressure than do those in the Quetico, requiring a more hands-on management approach. Second, while Minnesota is indeed the land of ten thousand lakes, Ontario is the land of hundreds of thousands of lakes. The MNR has higher priorities than to survey all the lakes in the Quetico. Consequently, while good survey data is available for the Boundary Waters lakes, few of the lakes on the Canadian side have been surveyed. This means that the fish species information in the Quetico index comes from a variety of sources, including official MNR data, as well as from my own experience, the reports of friends who frequent these lakes, and from fishing guides. It should not be considered as accurate as the information on the Boundary Waters lakes.

In the Boundary Waters index, if you see a fish species noted, and it isn't in parenthesis, those fish are really there. They've been caught in nets by DNR survey crews. That doesn't always mean those species are abundant. I suggest that you visit the MN DNR website for detailed information on a particular lake, which can reveal if the fish species is

only there in small numbers, or if it is a lake that you'd like to make a destination for some serious angling.

If the species column has nothing but hash marks in it, there is no information – either from the DNR or second hand, about the fish. If fish are noted, but in parenthesis with a question mark next to it, it means I've had reliable reports of that species being caught there, but those reports have not been confirmed by DNR lake survey. And occasionally you'll see "none" listed in that column. That means that the lake has been test-netted by the DNR, and there really are no fish present.

The lake indexes are really the meat of this book. Yes, the BWCAW lakes can now be found on-line, but this print version makes trip planning so much easier. The internet is wonderful, but it is not nearly as fast or as simple as merely paging through the index.

One of things I like to do when planning a canoe route is to break out my maps, a marking pen, and this book. Alongside every lake on our route, I write the fish species found in that lake – W for walleye, NP for northern pike, etc. I find this particularly handy because, if you've been on a canoe trip, you know that sometimes you don't always end up where you'd planned to go. You may have planned a lake trout trip to Lake X, but instead, because of a storm or a sprained ankle, you ended up on Lake Z. What's in Lake Z? Unless you put this book in your pack, you won't know. But with the fish information scribbled on your map, you'll be ready.

There are other fish species present in the Canoe Country that I didn't list in this guide, largely because they are not considered game fish. Suckers, for instance, have a wide distribution. Once, on a spring canoe trip, I found suckers spawning in a creek and scooped a couple up for dinner (fishing had been slow!). Suckers actually aren't bad eating when they come from cold, clear water. Feel free to disagree.

Some may wonder why I even included lake whitefish, as they aren't generally considered a game species. They were included for a couple of reasons, not the least of which is that you will occasionally catch them on lures, and, during an insect hatch, they can be a ball on a fly rod. Whitefish are delicious table fare as well. In addition, they are a fine forage fish for walleye, northern pike and lake trout. In my experience, lakes that contain whitefish yield bigger predators. That's a little tip you may want to file away in the back of your mind if you're looking for big lakers, big pike, or big walleye…

Bluegills, although technically a sunfish, are given special mention in the index because they tend to get quite a bit larger than green-eared or pumpkinseed sunfish, and therefore are more fun to catch, and make a better meal. If you see sunfish listed, it means that species other than bluegills have been found in the lake.

Perch are also included because, while here in walleye country they aren't often considered a game fish, many people travel to Minnesota and Ontario just to fish for perch. A near relative of walleye, they are every bit as good eating (maybe better), but unless they are of a size to make a meal, they can be just a nuisance. That said, there is some very fine perch fishing in the Canoe Country for those who are of a mind to pursue them.

You'll note that a few Quetico and border lakes include sturgeon as a listing. I don't know of anyone who goes into the Canoe Country to catch a sturgeon, but the fact remains that they are there, they can grow quite large and are a desirable food fish. Check the fishing regulations, though, to see if you can keep one, as size restrictions do apply.

Each wilderness has its own lake index. The BWCAW comes first, followed by the Quetico. Lakes in the BWCAW also have the county in which they are found. The three counties in which the BWCAW is located, from west to east, are St. Louis, Lake, and Cook.

Now get out your marker pen, your maps, and have fun planning that next canoe trip!

KEY

Fish species and abbreviations:

BC – Black Crappie
BG – Bluegill
BT – Brook Trout
LB – Largemouth Bass
LT – Lake Trout
M – Muskie
NP – Northern Pike
P – Yellow Perch
RT – Rainbow Trout
SA – Sauger
SB – Smallmouth Bass
SF – Sunfish
SP – Splake
ST – Sturgeon
W – Walleye
WF – Lake Whitefish
(—) – no information available

NOTE: *If a species is listed in parenthesis (NP?), it means that I had a reliable report of its presence, but it has not been confirmed by lake surveys or my own personal experience.*

BWCAW

Lake Name	County	Acres	Max. Depth	Species
Abinodji	L	39	33	NP
Abita	C	102	14	P
Ada	C	28	13	NP
Adams	L	590	84	BG, NP, W, WF
Adventure	L	51	9	NP, W
Afton	L	50	-	NP
Agamok	L	113	29	NP
Agawato	ST. L	39	58	NP, P
Agnes	ST. L	1,069	30	NP, P, SA, SB, W
Ahmakose	L	49	68	LT
Ahsub	L	58	78	BT, SB
Alder	C	506	72	LT, NP, SB, W
Alice	L	1,556	53	BG, NP, W, WF
Allen	C	49	12	SB, NP, P, W
Alpine	C	839	65	SB, NP, W, WF
Alruss	ST. L	28	48	BT
Alsike	L	30	16	NONE
Alton	C	1,039	72	SB, NP, W
Alworth	L	203	33	NP, P, W
Amber	L	135	27	BG, NP, P, W
Amini	L	23	-	--
Amoeber	L	386	110	SB, LT, W
Angleworm	ST. L	144	11	NP, P, W
Anit	L	12	19	NP
Annie	L	18	16	NP, SF, WF
Arch	ST. L	49	-	--
Arkose	L	21	37	P, SF
Arrow (North)	L	13	-	NP
Arrow (Mid.)	L	31	6	NP, P

Lake Name	County	Acres	Max. Depth	Species
Arrow (South)	L	22	12	NP, P
Ashdick	L	100	50	LB, NP
Ashigan	L	189	59	SB, P, SF
Baker	C	24	10	NP, P, W
Bald Eagle	L	1,238	36	BC, BG, NP, P, W, WF
Banadad	C	168	45	NP
Bandana	L	8	9	LB, NP, W
Barter	L	10	8	P, SF
Barto	C	95	40	--
Baskatong	L	67	6	NP
Basswood	L	22,722	111	BC, LB, NP, P, SB, SF, W, WF
Bat	C	80	110	LT
Batista	ST. L	77	-	--
Battle	ST. L	74	24	BG, LB, NP, W
Bear	ST. L	64	-	--
Bear Trap	ST. L	122	38	NP, SF, W
Beartrack	ST. L	168	55	P, SF
Beaver	L	237	76	BG, NP, W
Becoosin	L	52	17	P
Bench	C	26	16	BT
Benezie	L	59	27	BG, LB, NP, P
Besho	L	25	5	NONE
Beth	C	182	22	NP
Big Moose	ST. L	1,032	23	NP, SB, W
Big Rice	ST. L	420	5	NP, P
Bingshick	C	44	37	BT

BWCAW

BWCAW

Lake Name	County	Acres	Max. Depth	Species
Birch	L	711	34	BG, LB, NP, P, SB, W
Bog	L	249	16	NP, P, W
Bonnie	L	71	11	NP, P, SF
Boot	ST. L	313	27	NP, P, W
Boot	L	209	83	NP, SB, W
Bootleg	ST. L	340	26	BG, LB, NP, P
Boulder	L	238	54	NP, P
Boulder	ST. L	50	-	LB, NP, P
Bow	L	90	7	BG, NP, P
Bower (Lower) Trout	C	149	6	NP, SB, W
Boze	L	78	-	NP, W
Brant (Brandt)	C	104	80	NP, P
Bruin	L	50	30	NP, P
Brule	C	4,617	78	NP, SB, W
Buck	ST. L	228	19	NP, P, W
Bull	C	57	33	NP, P
Bullet	L	50	10	BG, NP, P, W
Bullfrog	L	62	26	NP, P
Burnt	C	327	23	NP, P, W
Cabin	L	67	3	NP, P
Cacabic	L	22	30	NP
Cache	L	42	15	NP, SB, W
Calf	C	15	18	P
Calico	L	11	20	P, SF
Cam	C	60	57	NP, P
Camdre	L	51	12	P
Camp	L	84	31	NP, P, SF, W

BWCAW

Lake Name	County	Acres	Max. Depth	Species
Canoe	C	94	40	P, SF, W
Canoe	L	18	30	P, SF
Canta	L	17	55	NP
Carey (Coxey)	ST. L	204	14	BG, LB, NP, SB, P, SF
Carl	C	45	20	NP, P
Caribou (near Moon Lake)	C	452	65	NP, SB, W, WF
Caribou (near Meeds Lake)	C	255	26	NP, P, W
Carol	L	96	16	BG, NP, P, W
Cash	C	109	80	LT, SF
Cattyman	L	17	9	NP, P, W
Chad	ST. L	266	18	BG, LB, NP, P
Cherokee	C	753	142	LT, NP
Cherry	L	147	90	LT, W
Clam	C	59	19	NP
Clam	L	18	10	P, SF
Clark	ST. L	66	44	BG, LB, NP, P
Clear	L	236	17	BC, BG, NP, P, W
Clearwater	C	1,325	130	LT, P, SB, SF
Clearwater	L	641	46	NP, P, WF
Clove	C	172	25	NP, P, SB, W, WF
Contentment	ST. L	44	50	NP
Cook County	L	43	38	SF
Cow	C	39	36	P
Crab	ST. L	541	57	LB, NP, SB, SF
Crab, Little	ST. L	61	15	LB, NP, SB
Crocodile	C	272	17	P, W

BWCAW

Lake Name	County	Acres	Max. Depth	Species
Crooked	C	233	66	LT, NP
Crooked	L & ST. L	7,941	165	BC, LB, NP, P, SA, SB, W, WF
Crow	C	37	6	NP, P, W
Crystal	C	205	80	LT, NP, SF, SB, W
Cummings	ST. L	1,121	41	BG, NP, P, SF, SB
Cypress (Ottertrack)	L	1,104	116	BG, NP, P, SF, SB, LT, W, WF
Daniels	C	508	90	LT, SB, P
Davis	C	353	64	LT, NP
Dawkins	C	68	19	NP, P, W
Deer	C	71	30	LB, NP, W
Dent	C	112	-	--
Devils Elbow	C	89	50	NP, SB, W, WF
Diana	L	44	13	NP, P, SF, W
Disappointment	L	867	54	LB, NP, P, SB, W
Dix	L	83	45	NP, SF
Dovre	ST. L	120	17	NP, P
Drumstick	L	19	-	--
Duck	ST. L	110	5	NONE
Dugout	C	25	8	NP, P, W
Duncan	C	481	130	LT, P, SB, SF
Dunn	C	90	60	LT, SF
Dutton	L	33	80	P
Eagle	C	72	14	NP, P, W
East Dawkins	C	48	15	NP, P, W
East Kerfoot	C	11	26	SF
East Pike	C	496	40	M, NP, SB, WF
East Pipe	C	106	12	NP, W

BWCAW

Lake Name	County	Acres	Max. Depth	Species
Echo	C	133	12	NP, SB, W
Eddy	L	122	95	LB, NP, P, WF
Edith	C	10	44	NP, P
Ella	C	53	6	NP, P
Ella Hall	L	372	28	BG, LB, NP, P, SF, SB
Elm	C	126	77	(LT?) NP
Elton	L	123	53	NP
Emerald	ST. L	67	34	P, SF
Ensign	L	1,408	30	BG, LB, NP, P, SB, W
Eskwagama	L	80	12	NP
Ester	L	388	110	LT, P, WF
Eugene	ST. L	166	64	NP, P, WF
Explorer	L	52	75	LT, P
Faith	L	25	15	NP
Fairy	ST. L	151	19	BG, NP, P, W
Fallen Arch	L	17	11	NP, P
Fall	L	2,173	32	BC, BG, NP, P, SB, W, WF
Fan	C	6	3	NONE
Fat	ST. L	102	50	LT
Fault	C	61	10	SF
Fay	C	66	62	BT, LT, SF
Fern	C	57	65	LT, NP
Ferne	L	130	8	NP, P, W
Finger	ST. L	287	60	NP, P, SB, W
Fire	L	96	30	BG, NP
Fish	L	92	30	NP, P, WF

BWCAW

Lake Name	County	Acres	Max. Depth	Species
Fishdance	L	180	50	BG, NP, P, SB, W, WF
Fisher	L	74	25	LB, P
Flame	C	55	22	NP, P
Found	L	60	38	BT
Four	L	655	25	BG, NP, P, W, WF
Fourtown	L	1,902	25	BG, NP, P, SB, W
Fox	ST. L	27	7	--
Fraser	L	811	105	LT, NP, W
Frederick	C	46	10	NP
French	C	112	130	LT, NP, P
Frog	L	42	38	LB, NP, P
Frost	C	236	88	LT, NP
Gabbro	L	896	50	BC, BG, NP, P, W
Gabimichigami	C	1,198	209	LT, NP, P
Gadwell (Gadwall)	C	20	52	BT
Gaskin	C	346	82	(LT?) NP, SB, W, WF
Ge-be-on-equat	ST. L	607	55	NP, P, SB, W, WF
Geraldine	ST. L	44	-	NP
Gerund	L	98	85	NP
Gibson	L	34	24	NP, P, W
Gift	L	38	35	NP, P, LW
Gijikiki	L	103	70	LT, P
Gillis	C	570	180	NP, P, LT
Glenmore	ST. L	56	8	BG, NP
Glimmer	ST. L	17	6	--

BWCAW

Lake Name	County	Acres	Max. Depth	Species
Gneiss	C	239	70	LT, NP, P, SB, SF, W, WF
Gogebic	C	70	61	BT
Good	L	177	51	BC, BG, LB, NP, P, W, WF
Gordon	C	139	95	(LT?) NP
Gowan	ST. L	158	13	NP, P, W
Grace	C	391	16	NP, P, W
Grandpa	C	120	55	NP, P, SF
Granite	C	120	45	NP, P, SB, W, WF
Green	ST. L	141	20	BG, NP, P, SF
Green	C	40	75	--
Grub	L	43	31	LB, SB, SF
Gulf	C	31	16	NP, P, SF
Gull	ST. L	169	13	NP, P, SF
Gull	L	503	31	NP, P, SB, W
Gump	C	13	11	--
Gun (near Fairy Lake)	ST. L	337	57	BG, NP, SB, W
Gun (near Lac La Croix)	ST. L	158	135	LT, P, SB
Handle	C	14	7	NP, P
Hanson	L	284	100	LT, NP, WF
Hassel	ST. L	62	5	BG, NP
Hatchet	L	126	40	NP, P, W
Hazel	C	98	7	NP, P
Hegman, North	ST. L	101	30	NP, P, SB, W
Hegman, South	ST. L	110	55	NP, P, SB
Henson	C	124	40	NP, P, SF, SB

Lake Name	County	Acres	Max. Depth	Species
Heritage	ST. L	184	43	NP, P, SB, W
Hilly	C	30	23	NP
Holt	L	106	73	NP, LT
Home	ST. L	85	24	NP, P, W
Homer	C	443	22	NP, P, SB, W
Hook	ST. L	83	13	NP, P
Hope	L	103	8	NP, P, W
Horse	L	681	25	BG, NP, P, W
Horsefish	L	51	-	NP
Horseshoe (near Vista Lake)	C	202	26	NP, SF, P, W
Horseshoe (near Lake Three)	L	194	40	BG, NP, P, W, WF
Howard	C	158	125	LT, NP
Hub	C	123	20	NP
Hudson	L	381	35	BG, NP, P, W, WF
Hula	L	121	4	NP, P, SF
Hustler	ST. L	272	74	BG, NP, P, SF
Huslter, Little	ST. L	67	70	BG, NP, SF
Ima	L	772	116	BG, LT, NP, P, W
Indiana	L	153	26	BG, NP, P, SB
Insula	L	2,597	63	NP, P, W, WF
Iron	ST. L	1,851	60	BC, NP, P, SA, SB, W
Isabella	L	1,257	19	BC, LB, NP, P, SF, W, WF
Jack	C	101	10	NP, P, W
Jackfish	L	209	18	NP
Jacob (Louis)	ST. L	23	52	BT

BWCAW

Lake Name	County	Acres	Max. Depth	Species
Jap (Paulson)	C	146	60	LT
Jasper	C	239	125	LT, SB, W, WF
Jenny	L	102	93	NP, P, WF
Jerry	C	77	47	(LT?) NP
Jimmy	C	27	5	NONE
Jitterbug	L	25	5	NP, P
John	C	191	20	NP, P, SB, W
Jordan	L	136	66	NP, P, W
Jug	L	32	6	NP
Juno	C	248	23	NP, P, W
Karl	C	105	70	LT, NP
Kawasachong	L	162	11	NP, P, W
Kawishiwi	L	400	12	NP, P, W
Kekakabic	L	1,620	195	LT, P
Kekakabic Pond 1	L	4	20	P
Kekakabic Pond 2	L	24	25	LT, NP
Kekakabic Pond 3	L	25	17	NP
Kelly	C	152	13	NP, P, SF, W
Kelsey	ST. L	130	22	NP, P, SF
Kelso	C	97	16	NP, P
Kettle	L	37	15	P, SF
Kiana	L	234	56	NP
Kingfisher	C	35	42	LT, P, W, WF
Kinogami	C	115	30	LB, M, NP, P, SB, W
Kiowa	C	32	29	P, SF
Kiskadinna	C	131	40	(LT? NP?)
Kivaniva	L	38	49	BG, NP, P, W

Lake Name	County	Acres	Max. Depth	Species
Knife	L	4,920	179	LT, NP, P, SB, W, WF
Knight	C	99	6	NP, P, SF
Koma	L	260	14	BG, NP, P, W, WF
Korb	ST. L	58	27	BG, NP, P, SB
La Pond	ST. L	176	4	(NP?)
Lac	C	55	20	NP, P
Lac La Croix	ST. L	34,070	168	BC, LT, NP, P, SA, SB, ST, W, WF
Lake of the Clouds	L	28	110	SF
Lamb	ST. L	80	18	NP, P
Larch	C	131	14	NP, P, W
Lily	C	22	51	NP, P
Link	L	37	34	NP, WF
Little Beartrack	ST. L	53	35	NP, SF
Little Caribou	C	58	18	NP, SB, P, W
Little Crab	ST. L	61	15	LB, NP, SB
Little Gabbro	L	154	26	NP, P, W
Little Hustler (Ruby)	ST. L	67	70	BG, NP, SF
Little Kekekabic (Kek Lake)	L	58	130	LT, P
Little Knife	L	700	184	LT, NP, SB, W, WF
Little Loon	ST. L	175	65	NP, SF, SB, W
Little Mayhew	C	35	31	NP, P, SF
Little North	C	98	23	NP, W
Little Rice	ST. L	110	5	P, SF
Little Rush	C	19	7	--

BWCAW

Lake Name	County	Acres	Max. Depth	Species
Little Saganaga	C	1,575	150	LT, NP, P
Little Shell	ST. L	84	40	BG, P, W
Little Trout (near Rum Lake)	C	123	56	LT
Little Trout (near Trout Lake)	ST. L	538	37	NP, P, SB, W
Little Vermilion	ST. L	1,288	52	BC, BG, NP, P, SA, SB, W, WF
Lizz	C	30	30	BT, P, SF
Long	C	140	24	NP, SF
Long Island	C	864	85	LT, NP
Loon	ST. L	3,101	70	BC, NP, P, SB, W, WF
Louis (Jacob)	ST. L	23	52	BT
Lower (Bower) Trout Lake	C	149	6	NP, P, SB, W
Lower Pauness	ST. L	156	36	NP, P, W
Lum	C	27	17	NP, P
Lunar	L	58	60	LT, SF
Lunetta	ST. L	88	14	BG, LB, NP, P, SB
Lux	C	47	21	NP, P
Lynx	ST. L	295	85	BG, NP, SB, W
Makwa	L	143	76	LT, NP, P
Malberg	L	404	37	BG, NP, P, W, WF
Maniwaki	L	97	10	--
Manomin	L	403	18	NP, P, SF
Maraboeuf	C	902	55	LT, NP, P, SB, W, WF
Marathon	L	31	11	NP, P

Lake Name	County	Acres	Max. Depth	Species
Marshall	C	51	16	NP, P, SB
Mavis	C	10	55	BT
Maxine	ST. L	37	21	BG, LB, NP, P SF
Meat	ST. L	25	24	NP, P
Meditation	C	28	31	BT
Meeds	C	337	41	NP, P, W
Merritt	ST. L	195	8	NP, P
Mesaba	C	201	65	LT, NP
Midas	L	20	50	NP
Middle Cone	C	73	30	NP, SB, W
Midget	C	24	25	NP, P
Misplaced	C	25	18	--
Misquah	C	60	60	LT
Missing Link	C	40	25	BT
Moon	C	145	30	NP, P, SB, W
Moose (near North Fowl)	C	1,005	113	LT, P, SB, W, WF
Moose (near Ely)	L	1,211	65	BG, LB, NP, P, SF, SB, W
Moosecamp	L	190	16	BG, NP, W
Mora	C	205	40	NP
Morgan	C	82	46	NP
Morris	C	62	22	NP, SF, SB, W
Mountain	C	2,088	210	LT, SB
Mud	L	179	16	NP, P
Mudro	ST. L	95	76	NP, P, W
Mueller	L	24	36	NP, P
Mule	ST. L	47	10	--

BWCAW

Lake Name	County	Acres	Max. Depth	Species
Mulligan	C	30	62	BT, NP
Muskeg	L	132	7	NP, P
Muskeg	C	37	15	--
Muskrat	L	24	18	P, W
Muzzle	L	72	--	--
Nabek	L	48	65	NONE
Nawakwa	L	88	9	NP, P
Neesh	ST. L	39	6	NP, P
Neewin	ST. L	100	15	NP, P
Neglige	L	28	58	BT
Newfound	L	604	45	BG, LB, NP, SB, W
Newton	L	500	47	BG, BC, NP, P, SB, W, WF
Night Hawk	C	18	11	NP, W
Nina Moose	ST. L	430	6	NP, P, SB, W
Niswi	ST. L	119	18	NP, P
North (near Gunflint Lake)	C	2,695	125	LT, NP, P, SB, W
North (near Lac La Croix)	ST. L	99	10	BC, NP, P, SB, SF, W
North (Upper) Cone	C	86	55	NP, SB, W
North Fowl	C	1,020	10	NP, P, W
North Kerfoot	C	-	-	--
North Temperance	C	178	50	NP, P, W
North Wilder	L	99	25	BG, NP, P, W
Norway	ST. L	58	37	NP, P

Lake Name	County	Acres	Max. Depth	Species
Ogishkemuncie	L	701	75	LT, NP, P, W, WF
Omega (Ogema)	C	196	77	NP
One	L	876	57	BG, NP, P, W, WF
One Island	C	19	25	NP, P
Oriniak	ST. L	762	17	BG, NP, P, W
Otter	ST. L	78	17	BG, NP, SB
Ottertrack (Cypress)	L	1,104	116	BG, NP, P, SB, SF, W, WF
Owl	C	81	70	LT, P
Oyster	ST. L	714	130	LT, NP, P, SB
Paddle	C	16	16	NP, P, SB, W
Pagami	L	41	7	BG, NP, P, W
Pan	L	100	59	BG, NP, P, W
Panhandle	L	8	22	NP, P
Parent	L	326	50	NP, SB, W
Partridge	C	109	80	LT, SF
Paulson (Jap)	C	146	60	LT
Pekan	ST. L	36	23	P, SF
Pemmican	C	28	51	BT
Perent	L	1,800	28	NP, P, W, WF
Peter	C	259	120	LT
Peterson	C	88	15	NP, P, SB, W
Phantom	ST. L	52	10	NP, P
Phoebe	C	625	25	NP, P, W
Pickle	L	97	22	(NP?)
Pie	C	75	10	(NP?)
Pierz	C	88	28	SP
Pietro	L	339	31	NP, SF

BWCAW

Lake Name	County	Acres	Max. Depth	Species
Pillsberry	C	66	20	--
Pine (near Trout Lake)	ST. L	912	18	NP, P, SF, W
Pine (near McFarland Lake)	C	2,257	113	LT, NP, P, SB, W, WF
Pipe	C	300	33	NP, P
Pocket	ST. L	226	27	NP, P, W
Polly	L	479	21	NP, P, SB, SF, W
Portage	L	69	45	NP, SB
Pose	L	76	12	BG, NP, P
Powell	C	51	75	LT
Pow-wow	L	21	42	NP, P
Prayer	C	43	19	NP
Profit	ST. L	15	12	P, SF
Quadga	L	248	35	NP, P, SF, W
Rabbit	L	104	105	LT
Ram	C	67	40	LT, RT
Ramshead	ST. L	480	10	NP, P, SF
Range	L	82	19	BC, BG, LB, NP, P, SF, (W?)
Range Line	ST. L	87	52	(LT?)
Rat	C	56	5	P, SB, SF
Rattle	C	45	30	NP, P
Raven	L	205	56	LT
Red Rock	C	353	64	LT, NP, SB, W, WF
Reward	C	21	14	NP, P
Rib	C	82	10	(NP?)

Lake Name	County	Acres	Max. Depth	Species
Rice (off Isabella River)	L	206	5	W, NP
Rice (Kenue)	ST. L	37	27	NP
Rifle	L	36	18	NP
Ritual	ST. L	64	40	(NP?)
Rock Island	L	55	21	NP
Rocky	C	76	35	NP
Rocky	ST. L	116	40	NP, P, SF
Roe	L	70	7	(NP?) SF
Rog	C	51	40	BT, SB
Romance	C	149	32	(NP?)
Rose	C	1,315	90	LT, P, SB, W, WF
Rove	C	78	30	P, SF, SB, W
Roy	C	61	45	NP
Ruby	ST. L	39	49	(LT?) (NP?)
Rush (near Banadad Lake)	C	274	54	NP
Rush (near Iron Lake)	ST. L	119	10	NP, P, SB, W
Saca	ST. L	73	18	NP, SB
Saganaga	C	17,593	280	LT, NP, P, SB, W, WF
Sagus	L	172	37	NP, P, W
Sandpit	L	61	53	BG, LB, NP, SB
Sawbill	C	765	45	NP, P, SB, W
Schlamm	ST. L	65	6	BG, NP, P
Seagull	C	4,032	145	LT, NP, P, SB, SF, W, WF
Sedative	L	85	27	(NP)?

BWCAW

Lake Name	County	Acres	Max. Depth	Species
Seed	L	89	10	NP, W
Sema	L	86	72	LT
Shadow	C	14	23	SF
Shell	ST. L	484	15	BG, LB, NP, P, SF, SB, W
Shepo	L	52	17	NP, W
Shrike	C	26	11	NP, P
Silica	ST. L	49	16	BG, NP, SF, SB
Sinneeg	ST. L	157	32	NP, P, SF, W
Skidway	C	18	8	NP, P, W
Skindance	L	58	52	NP, P
Skipper	C	108	30	NP, P, W
Skoop	C	9	17	--
Skull	L	28	38	BT
Slim (off Burntside Lake)	ST. L	312	49	NP, P, SF, SB, W
Slim (near Lac La Croix)	ST. L	121	42	NP, P
Smite	L	46	22	BG, NP, W
Smoke	C	158	20	NP, P, SB, W
Snipe	C	112	90	--
Snowbank	L	4,273	150	LT, NP, P, SB, W
Sock	C	20	23	BT
South (near North Lake	C	1,190	140	LT, SB
South (near Slim Lake)	ST. L	35	10	NP, P, SF
South (Lower) Cone	C	67	21	NP, SB, W

Lake Name	County	Acres	Max. Depth	Species
South Farm	L	618	30	BC, BG, NP, P, SB, W
South Hope	L	55	9	NP, P, W
So. Temperance	C	204	24	NP, P, SB, W
South Wilder	L	61	36	BG, NP, W
Spaulding	C	53	36	NONE
Spice	L	24	27	NP, P, SF
Spider	L	33	55	(NP?)
Splash	L	97	18	BG, NP, P, W
Spoon	L	223	85	NP, P
Square	L	127	7	NP, P, W
Squire	C	82	7	NP, P
Steep	ST. L	86	40	NP
Stem	C	43	34	NP
Sterling	ST. L	180	--	--
Strup	L	79	105	(LB?) (LT?)
Stuart	ST. L	776	40	NP, P, W
Sucker	L	382	31	BG, NP, P, SB, W, WF
Sunday	ST. L	124	--	(NP?)
Sunhigh	C	54	14	(NP?)
Sunlow	C	31	6	--
Swamp	C	181	10	NP, P, W
Swan	C	180	122	(LT?) NP, SB, W, WF
Swing	L	10	13	NONE
Table	C	20	5	NONE
Takucmich	ST. L	327	150	BG, LT, SB
Tenor	C	20	11	NP, P, SB, W

BWCAW

Lake Name	County	Acres	Max. Depth	Species
Tepee	C	96	22	NP, P
Tesoker	ST. L	24	37	BG, LB, P
Thirty-three	L	31	9	(NP?)
Thomas	L	1,471	110	BG, LT, NP, P, W
Three	L	881	37	BG, NP, P, W
Three Eagle	L	60	--	--
Thumb	ST. L	52	55	NP, W
Thunder	ST. L	169	52	(NP?) (W?)
Tickle	L	43	61	(NP?) P, SF
Tin Can Mike	L	147	29	BG, NP, SB, W
Tobacco	C	13	9	NP, P
Toe	ST. L	166	57	NP, SB, SF, W
Topaz	L	130	70	LT, SB
Topper	C	47	28	BT
Tornado	L	25	7	NP, P
Totem	L	15	19	NP, P
Town	C	79	72	LT
Trader	L	54	10	P, SF
Trail	L	62	--	(NP?) (W?)
Treasure	L	79	53	--
Tremolo	L	31	20	(NP?)
Trident	L	90	14	BG, NP, P, SF, SB, W
Trillium	ST. L	36	35	(LB?) (SF?)
Trout	ST. L	7,425	98	LT, NP, SB, W
Trygg	ST. L	25	35	BT
Tucker	C	168	42	NP, W
Turtle	L	337	10	NP, P
Tuscarora	C	833	130	LT, NP, P

Lake Name	County	Acres	Max. Depth	Species
Two	L	481	35	BG, NP, P, W, WF
Upper Pauness	ST. L	162	14	NP, P, W
Vale	C	24	34	BT
Vaseau	C	10	10	NONE
Vera	L	245	55	(LB?) W
Vern	C	142	42	NP, SB, W
Vernon	C	233	101	LT, NP, SB, W, WF
Virgin	C	56	40	NONE
Vista	C	222	47	NP, P, W
Wager	L	10	11	NP, P
Wagosh	ST. L	49	--	--
Washte	L	84	7	P
Watap	C	202	45	P, SF, SB, W
Watonwan	L	59	25	NP, P, W
Wee	C	13	34	BT
Weird	C	33	6	NP, P, W
Wench	C	24	59	BT
West Bearskin	C	494	78	BG, LT, NP, P, SB
West Fern	C	75	60	LT
West Kerfoot	C	24	15	BG, LB, SF
West Otto	C	61	55	(W?)
West Pike	C	715	120	LT, SB
West Pipe	C	17	6	NP
Western	ST. L	41	12	NP, P, W
Whack	C	34	27	NP
Whale	C	21	10	NP, P
Whip	C	35	9	NP, P
Whipped	C	62	--	(NP?)

BWCAW

BWCAW

Lake Name	County	Acres	Max. Depth	Species
Whisker	C	24	5	NONE
White Feather	ST. L	105	6	(NP?)
Whiz	L	24	44	BG, NP, P
Winchell	C	826	160	LT, NP, WF
Wind	L	1,009	32	BG, LB, NP, P, SF, W
Wine	C	257	65	LT
Wisini	L	129	137	(LB?) (LT?)
Witness	L	41	19	P, W
Wonder	C	85	10	(NP?)
Wood	L	643	21	BG, NP, P, (SB?), W
Yodeler	ST. L	44	--	--
Zenith	C	20	20	--
Zephyr	C	122	40	NP, SB, W, WF
Zoo	C	90	26	NP

Lake Name	Acres	Species
Agnes	7,397	LT, NP, P, SB, W, WF
Allen	229	NP, W
Alice	1,269	NP
Anchor	84	LB
Antoine	568	LT, NP
Anubis	153	NP, SB, W
Argo	2,364	LT, NP, SB
Art	247	NP, W
Badwater	477	LT, NP, P, W
Baird	175	NP, W
Ballard	279	LB, NP, SA, SB, W
Baptism	563	NP, W
Bart	393	LB, NP, P, SB, SF, W
Basswood	22,722	BC, LB, NP, P, SB, SF, W, WF
Batchewaung	2,638	LT, NP, SB, W
Bearpelt	573	NP, P, W
Beaverhouse	4,945	LT, NP, P, SB, W
Beg	225	NP, SB, W
Bell	153	BC, SF
Bentpine	1,015	NP, P, SB, W
Berniece	392	NP, W
Birch	711	LT, NP, SB, W
Bird	281	NP, SB, W
Bisk	200	NP, P, SB, W
Bit	104	NP, W
Bock	138	LT
Brent	2,159	LB, LT, NP, SB, W

QUETICO

QUETICO

Lake Name	Acres	Species
Brewer	252	LB, NP, SB, W
Buckingham	627	LT, NP, W
Bud	276	NP, SB, W
Burke	650	LB, LT, NP, SB, W
Burntside	1,297	LT, NP, SB, W
Burt	1749	LB, LT, NP, SB, W
Cache	1,089	LT, NP, SB
Cairn	422	NP, SB, W
Camel	477	NP, W
Carp	1,101	LT, NP, P, SB, W
Cecil	138	SB
Ceph	42	NP, SB, SF, W
Chatterton	692	NP, SB, W
Cirrus	5,224	BC, LT, NP, SB, W
Clair	168	NP, W
Cone	160	LT, SB
Conk	279	NP
Conmee	1,242	LB, NP, SB, W
Crooked	7,941	BC, LB, NP, P, SA, SB, W, WF
Cub	163	NP, W
Cutty	462	NP, SB, W
Dack	476	LT, NP, W
Dahlin	173	NP, SB
Darky	1,230	BC, LT, NP, SF, SB, W
Dart	110	SB

QUETICO

Lake Name	Acres	Species
Deer	120	SB, W
Delahey	699	NP, W
Dell	62	LB, NP, P
Dore	731	LT, NP
Draper	422	LT, NP, W
East	212	NP, SB, W
Edge	212	NP
Elizabeth	326	NP, W
Elk	306	LT, SB
Emerald	640	LT, P
Ferguson	1,010	LT, NP
Fern	325	NP, SB, W
Fred	793	NP, SB, W
French	746	LT, NP, P, SB, W
Glacier	306	LT, SB, W
Goodier	136	LT
Gratton	64	LB, P
Grey	79	LB, SB
Heronshaw	257	NP, SB, W
Howard	215	NP
Hurlburt	296	NP, SB, W
Hurn	280	SB
Iron	1,851	BC, NP, P, SA, SB, W
Isabella	128	LB, NP, P, SB, W
Jack	185	NP, P, W
Jasper	205	SB, W
Jean	2,176	BG, LB, LT, NP, P, SB, W
Jeff	800	NP, W

QUETICO

Lake Name	Acres	Species
Jesse	800	NP, W
Joyce	973	LT, NP, SB, W
Kahshahpiwi	1,203	LT, NP, SB, W
Kasakokwog	1,902	LT, NP, P, SB, W
Kawnipi	9,035	LT, NP, P, SB, W
Keats	358	NP, SB, W
Keefer	538	LT, NP, SB, W
Keewatin	158	NP, SB, W
Kenney	257	NP, W
Kett	250	LT, NP, SB
Knife	4,920	LT, NP, P, SB, W, WF
Lac La Croix	34,070	BC, LT, NP, P, SA, SB, ST, W, WF
Lakin	190	NP, P
Lemay	385	NP, W
Lilypad	62	NP, SB, W
Little Knife	1,680	LT, NP, SB, W
Little Newt	59	LB
Little Pine	136	NP
Little Roland	54	NP, P, SF, SB
Lonely	976	NP, SB, W
Louisa	1,773	LT, NP, SB
Lynx	86	NP
Mack	1,882	LB, NP, P, W
Maria	299	NP, W
Marj	563	LT, SB
Meadows	183	BC, LB, SB
Metacryst	158	NP, SB, W
Middle Roland	158	NP, SB, P

Lake Name	Acres	Species
Milt	170	LB, LT, SB
Minn	1,146	NP, P, SB, W
Montgomery	309	NP, W
Murdock	731	NP, W
McAlpine	743	LT, NP, W
McAree	2,183	LT, NP, P, SB, W
McDougall	943	LT, NP
McEwen	1,267	LT, NP, SB, W
McIntyre	1,497	LT, NP, SB, W
McKenzie	3,995	LT, NP, P, SB
McNaught	133	BG, LB, NP, SB
McNiece	153	LT, NP
Nan	150	NP, SB, W
Nest	165	LT, NP
No Man	62	LT, NP, W
Noon	163	LB, SB
Oliphaunt	1,367	LT, NP, SB, W
Omeme	328	NP, W
Oriana	963	LB, LT, NP, W
Other Man	442	LT, NP, SB, W
Ottertrack	1,104	BG, NP, P, SB, SF, W, WF
Paulette	175	LB, SB
Pickerel	7,314	LT, NP, P, SA, SB, W
Plough	153	LT, NP
Poacher	306	LT, NP
Point	101	NP, SB
Pond	190	LT, NP, SB
Poohbah	3,336	LT, NP, SB, P, W

QUETICO

Lake Name	Acres	Species
Pulling	79	LB, SB
Quetico	10,535	LT, NP, SB, SF, P, W
Ram	198	LT, NP
Rawn	830	LT, NP, P, SB, W
Robin	200	LB, NP, P, SF, W
Robinson	1,030	LB, LT, NP, P, SB, W
Roland	568	LT, NP, P, SB, W
Rouge	163	NP, SB, W
Russell	2,445	NP, SB, W
Saganaga	17,593	LT, NP, P, SB, W, WF
Saganagons	5,350	LT, NP, SB, W
Sarah	2,848	LB, LT, NP, SB, W
Sark	701	LT, NP, SB, W
Shade	435	LB, LT, NP, P, SB, W
Shelley	741	NP, SB, W
Sheridan	230	LT, NP
Side	52	LT, NP
Silence	570	LB, LT, NP, P, SB, W
Slate	180	NP, SB, W
Smally	--	LB, SF
Smudge	111	NP, W
Snow	229	NP, W
Soho	670	LT, NP, W
Sturgeon	10,058	LT, NP, SA, SB, ST, W, WF

Lake Name	Acres	Species
Sucker	--	NP, W
Sultry	153	NP, SB, W
Summer	160	LT, NP, SB, W
Sunday	1,037	LB, LT, NP, SF, SB, W
Suzanette	691	LB, SB, W
Tanner	985	NP, SB, W
Ted	309	LT, NP, SB, W
That Man	385	BC, LT, NP, SB, W
This Man	776	BC, LT, NP, SF, W
Trail	229	NP, W
Trant	198	LB, W
Trousers	504	NP
Tuck	691	LT, NP, SB, W
Veron	655	NP, W
Walter	776	LT, NP, SB, W
West	101	LB, NP, W
Wet	741	NP, SB, W
Wicksteed	1,489	NP, P, SF, SB, W
Wildgoose	240	NP, W
William	672	NP, SB, W
Williams	444	NP, SB, W
Wink	857	LT, NP, SB, W
Wolseley	3,278	LT, NP, SB, W
Woodside	286	W
Yeh	89	LB, NP, SF, W
Your	487	NP, SF, W
Yum Yum	128	LT, NP, SB, W

QUETICO